Shoplifting
Controlling a Major Crime

Shoplifting
Controlling a Major Crime

D. P. Walsh

M

© D. P. Walsh 1978

All rights reserved. No part of this publication may be reproduced or transmitted, in any form or by any means, without permission.

First published 1978 by
THE MACMILLAN PRESS LTD
London and Basingstoke
Associated companies in Delhi Dublin
Hong Kong Johannesburg Lagos Melbourne
New York Singapore and Tokyo

Printed in Great Britain by
Redwood Burn Limited
Trowbridge & Esher

British Library Cataloguing in Publication Data

Walsh, D P
   Shoplifting.
   1. Shoplifting – Great Britain
   I. Title
   364.1'62   HV6665.G7

ISBN 0–333–23752–8
ISBN 0–333–23855–9   Pbk.

This book is sold subject to the standard conditions of the Net Book Agreement.

The paperback edition of this book is sold subject to the condition that it shall not, by way of trade or otherwise, be lent, re-sold, hired out, or otherwise circulated without the publisher's prior consent in any form of binding or cover other than that in which it is published and without a similar condition including this condition being imposed on the subsequent purchaser.

For Ann

Contents

List of Tables	ix
Acknowledgements	xi
Introduction	xiii

1 Shops and Shopping — 1

    The development of shops — 1
    Changes in shop type over time — 8
    The role of the shop assistant — 12
    The social significance of the shopping custom — 17

2 Shoplifting — 23

    Nine questions for the shoplifter — 31
    Motives for shoplifting — 35
    Community response to shoplifting — 47
    Community disposal of shoplifters — 52

3 Shoplifting in Exeter — 57

    Extent and concentration of shoplifting offences — 61
    Offender characteristics — 67
    Victim reaction — 76
    Means of preventing shoplifting — 84

4 Conclusions — 90

    Preventing shoplifting — 107
    Envoi — 111

Notes and References — 113
Bibliography — 117
Index — 121

List of Tables

1	Number of retail establishments	9
2	Numbers of shoplifting offences known to the police	29
3	Area distribution of shoplifting offences known to the police	30
4	Distribution of shops in the sample	59
5	Size of shops in the sample	59
6	Proportions in the offender sample	60
7	Area distribution of known shoplifting offences (Exeter)	61
8	Date of last offence of shoplifting (shopkeeper sample)	62
9	Premises where offence occurred (offences known to the police)	63
10	Rate of detection by shop type (offences known to the police)	64
11	Monthly distribution of offences (offences known to the police)	65
12	Daily distribution of offences (offences known to the police)	65
13	Time of day when offence occurred (offender sample)	66
14	Sex and age of offenders (offender sample)	67
15	Ages of shoplifters (offences known to the police)	68
16	Occupation of offenders (offender sample)	69
17	Preference for isolation or ganging among shoplifting offenders (offences known to the police)	70

x *List of Tables*

18	Goods stolen (offender sample)	72
19	Objects reported as most commonly stolen (shopkeeper sample)	73
20	Amount stolen in pounds sterling by detected shoplifters in Devon and Cornwall (1975)	74
21	Previous offences of shoplifters (offender sample)	76
22	Method of disposal of offenders (offender sample)	77
23	Action taken to prevent shoplifting (shopkeeper sample)	78
24	Opinions as to why people shoplift (shopkeeper sample)	81
25	How shoplifting might be stopped (shopkeeper sample)	82

Figure 1	Constraints in the crime of shoplifting	98
Figure 2	Constraints in crimes of theft	105

Acknowledgements

I should like especially to acknowledge the help given to me in this study by Detective Chief Superintendent P. J. Sharpe, Q.P.M., C.P.M., Chief Superintendent A. D. G. Wallen, Inspector A. Jordan, and Mr Rockett (Statistical Officer), all of Devon and Cornwall Constabulary. I am most grateful to them for their more than generous assistance.

Acknowledgement of permission to make use of material from copyright works is made to the following:

Maurice Temple Smith, London, from *The Victorian Underworld*, by K. Chesney, 1972; Tavistock Publications, London, from *Sociology and the Stereotype of the Criminal*, by D. Chapman, 1968; Sweet & Maxwell, London, from *Criminal Investigation*, by R. L. Jackson, 1962; Baillière, Tindall & Cassell, London, from *Aids to Psychiatry*, by W. S. Dawson, 1946, and from *Clinical Psychiatry*, by E. Slater and M. Roth, 1970; Holt Rinehart & Winston Inc., Hinsdale, Illinois, from *Consumer Behaviour*, by J. F. Engel *et al.*, 1968; The Dorsey Press, Illinois, from *Crime, Correction and Society*, by E. H. Johnson, 1974; Routledge & Kegan Paul Ltd, London, from *A History of Shopping*, by D. Davis, 1966; Chief Constable's Office, Devon and Cornwall Constabulary, from *The Annual Report of the Chief Constable*, 1975; Eyre Methuen Ltd, London, from 'Excerpts from Sir Samuel Romilly's Diary 1807–1818', in *English Historical Documents*, vol. XI, *1783–1832*, ed. A. Aspinall and E. A. Smith, 1959; McGraw-Hill Book Company, New York, from *Handbook of Consumer Motivation*, by E. Dichter, © Ernest Dichter, 1964; Penguin Books Ltd, Harmondsworth, from *The Complete Guide to Retail Management*, by A. Fiber, © Alan Fiber, 1972; The Controller of Her Majesty's Stationery Office, from *Criminal Statistics (England and Wales)*, and from *Annual Abstract of Statistics, 1975*, table 294.

Introduction

The main reason for producing this study has been a growing and developing interest in the role of victims in relation to crime, which has in turn led on to subsidiary interests. Isolating the three chief components in any crime that occurs consists of distinguishing the criminal (his personality, his characteristics and the cultural context within which he occurs) from the criminal event (as the occurrence of an act which is proscribed by the criminal law, which takes place in a particular place at a particular time, executed by a particular method which may be commonly used by a number of people), usually involving a victim, who may be either singular (just one person) or plural (a number of people, perhaps an organisation or a firm).

Studies which have tried to isolate 'causes of crime' have perhaps failed for reasons which are intellectually endemic to the subject matter of criminology, which is intrinsically a tangled skein which cannot be sectioned by using just one tool or approach. More particularly, such studies have obviously failed as a result of their focus on criminals alone, as if they were semi-autistic beings. The emotional reaction which follows any crime usually produces a pressure to do just this of course, to examine the criminal to the exclusion of other features which surround him, or which he may be linked with. Ultimately, criminology must deal with the type and form of the criminal event, and the relationship of the victim as well as, and together with, characteristics or qualities of criminals.

Very little is known about the victims of crime for various reasons, principally, perhaps, access to representative groups. Victims have a role which includes failing to inhibit particular crimes, and it is highly likely that most of them do not become victims solely through the operation of chance alone. For reasons which are not yet clear they have been selected by criminals as targets, whereas other possibles have been rejected, perhaps as being in some sense unsuitable. Criminology needs to know, amongst other things, much more about the individuals deemed unsuitable as victims, as well as why it is that particular people become victims. It is also true that inasmuch as criminologists may see themselves as having some loosely defined obligation to involve themselves in crime prevention, without a victim a crime cannot occur, and this obvious truth might pinpoint an alternative way of tackling crime prevention.

If the victim is not present, or will not for some reason collaborate or co-operate with the criminal (without realising the significance or outcome of what he has started to involve himself with), or if the victim reacts unexpectedly in a way that the criminal could not have predicted, then the majority of criminal enterprises must fail. The criminal in preparing to engage in crime has already made certain tacit assumptions about the probable behaviour of the victim, and organised his own behaviour to match this. As in other aspects of social life, the criminal prefers to operate within a framework of predictability and constancy of expectations: not to think he knows the future puts him at a disadvantage. Without predictability, few crimes occur, or must fail. This would happen for example if the potential victim of the would-be crime refuses to participate in the charade which might have finally been categorised as a breach of the criminal law through, let us say, taking a different route while carrying the weekly takings to the bank.

In so far, then, as criminologists do have some sort of obligation to suggest means of crime prevention, it is the case that an easier way to formulate the problem is not to focus solely on attempting to suppress criminal activity *per se*, through the use of direct technical counter-measures (such as bigger locks), but instead to consider focusing on victim prevention, which would logically achieve the same objective and do this more easily since the behaviour of potential victims is more easily guided than is the behaviour of criminals. That is accepting the premise that most crimes can only occur if there is a suitable victim. Schur (1965) has ably discussed the relatively few crimes without victims in a book of the same name.

Theft in general, and the reasons why people should steal from others, is a fascinating area to consider. Usually attempts to untangle it analytically have revolved around the examination of thieves alone, most frequently being even more limited through only looking at captured thieves and their qualities and reactions, and expecting to find patterns or clusters in their activity which will allegedly show why crimes are committed. This of course is as logically fallacious as assuming that an examination in a laboratory of a lead weight removed from a grandfather clock will facilitate an understanding of Time.

Self-evidently there are certain things about criminals which we need to know, and it is perfectly valid to scan for patterns and clusters in classifications derived from these things. However, and this is still a much neglected area in criminology, it is also necessary to ask questions about the cultural context within which crimes occur, and to ask why some people are selected as victims rather than others.

I have decided to examine the crime of shoplifting as an illustration of this approach, reasoning that studies so far produced have tended to focus exclusively on the shoplifting offender and his personal motivation, and for that matter his personality, rather than on the victims of shoplifting, and the crime-form proper, how the criminal event is occurring, not just in terms of *modus operandi* but also in terms of the location of the criminal event in social space.

With shoplifting, taken as a sub-type of theft generally, there is every reason to suppose that there are thousands of 'causes of crime'. People can do this thing for very many different reasons, in the same way that they can ride a bicycle for many different reasons. How much further is our knowledge of this (or for that matter any other crime) likely to be advanced by attempting, and of necessity failing, to produce a complete list of all the reasons why members of an advanced and complex industrial society, plentifully stocked with transferable private property, might from time to time steal some of this from other members? I am arguing that we might want to take this as far as we could, and then turn to other avenues for insights, rather than doggedly adhering to just one approach disguised in a variety of novel ways. Even if the list of reasons could be produced, it would be staggering in its length, and would very probably disclose little other than that humans can do things for countless different reasons.

What I have aimed to do in the study that follows is to try and take the crime-form of shoplifting to pieces, and to examine other inputs which feed into it which have hitherto not been discussed, in the process deliberately ignoring for the most part the motives of the offender in order to see how far our knowledge of this crime is furthered through concentrating on event and victim. If we were just searching for motives, then the task would be more complicated than the one I have described, not least because the examination must be retrospective. It must deal with the past as recorded, imperfectly, by the memory of the criminal, who can and may misrepresent himself and his motivations and actions in part due to legal pressures. For such reasons I make no apologies for deliberately refusing to deal with shoplifting offenders as a central focus, choosing instead to examine the scene of the crime, the criminal event and the victim.

To understand modern shoplifting as it now occurs, it will be necessary to place it in its cultural setting. We must consider how and why shops in the particular form that they take in this society have developed over time, and what the significance of shopping generally is, as a social phenomenon, and who actually engages in it and how. It is also necessary to consider the community reaction to theft generally, and the social and moral responses the community makes to it, as well as how the crime of shoplifting itself has changed over time (if indeed it really has), including such ancillary questions as how social response to it has altered and so on.

In talking about a crime-form it is crucial to put it into chronological perspective too. It is not possible to comment usefully on a current level of a crime without also considering what future levels *could* be and why, and what past levels *were* and why. Only in this way is it possible to see the how and why of the present. A present orientation alone is not going to be helpful, since, leaving aside pressure to react emotionally, it would give no perspective on what the rate and rationale for that crime was, and what it could grow to be over time. More significantly, pure present orientation involves a complete abrogation of the scientific right to predict.

In the case of examining the history of a crime, both social and economic, there are difficulties of access to reliable data: information may have been reported initially in a distorted or condensed form, or in some way rationalised by the original author; in the case of making estimates about probable future trends one might have thought that there was minimal hard data. This latter does indeed seem to be the case as long as the investigator persists in concentrating on the offender alone, which is a selected choice rather than a data-determined one. The fact that it may be difficult to obtain such information does not mean that we should not at least *try*.

Speaking generally, if the crime, taken to include victim, event and offender, is the focus, then the peripheral inputs to this focus must be examined closely to shed light on the final outcome. The alternative is to try and examine the outcome without reference to the inputs and the total cultural context within which it occurs. The result of this is that such an examination tends to focus more and more exclusively on the characteristics of the offender, and ultimately tails off in unsupported generalisations.

1

Shops and Shopping

The development of shops

The origin of the modern European shop as we now know it, as an economic and architectural entity, is to be found in the medieval fair. Fairs in medieval times spontaneously occurred and reappeared cyclically on days of special festivities. They involved entertainment, gossip, friction, magic, and especially gave people the opportunity to buy and sell, particularly food and livestock. They were the historical precursors of markets, which served the same economic purpose in a more specialised and efficient way. Markets in turn were the forerunners of early shops, which have subsequently mutated dramatically into the elaborate and costly shops of today. There is a large literature on the history, appearance and development of shops, and extremely useful expositions are contained in Davis (1966), Willan (1970), Edwards (1933), Levy (1947) and Somake and Hellberg (1956).

In the medieval fair or street market there is every reason to suppose that theft was commonplace and very difficult to avoid for the merchant. A market represents a large collection of accessible and concentrated transferable property which is privately owned and privately ownable, but only temporarily on display. Hence it becomes a prime target for the thief. The medieval market stallholder who neglected to realise that theft was highly likely would have simply gone out of business as a result of his folly. Gradually, over the years, as street markets became more permanent and more organised, there developed a specialised method of buying and selling; a ritual in fact, which among other things was specifically constructed to reduce the probability of successful theft occurring. So we find that it becomes conventional for the customer to stand on one side of a wooden board or marble slab, and for the seller to stand on the other. It is a similar convention that the customer does not cross the counter or pass around the end of it. Doing so without invitation becomes an open declaration of intent to steal. Further, the market stall-owner learned not to leave his stock and his stall unattended, even for an instant, whatever the reason. To do so would be to give an alert and watchful thief the chance he was waiting for.

The few remaining street market stalls of today are the direct descendants of medieval ones, where now, as in medieval times, the owner expects theft, and sees it as a tiresome but ordinary routine part of his life. The modern market stallholder never leaves his stall unsupervised, and prefers not to have to work it alone, usually having at least one other person with him, and as many extra as he can get for busy times, such as weekends. It is not that he does not trust people, it is just that past experience indicates that they steal when they can. The stall itself is shaped so that the people working it can easily prevent a would-be thief from stealing. The very term 'stall' shows this, implying as it does a cubicle which can be readily overseen.[1] Such a stall is purely functional. It is a place to purchase, not to linger, and as far as the thief is concerned it is relatively impregnable.

As markets became regular and permanent features in the medieval town, predictable events around which much of social and economic life was organised, occupying the same place in the same area, so eventually the stall open to the elements was gradually rebuilt on a firmer, more substantial basis. It was given a proper roof and walls, and customers found that instead of having to do business standing in the rain they now walked in through a door into what had translated itself from a stall into an early shop. As the process of change slowly occurred, and as the market-place became more fixed and less peripatetic, the theft problem remained unaltered, since the goods were still concentrated prior to sale. With the street market, the potential thief was well aware that there were gathered together in one place large quantities of saleable and transferable stock and property; he must have been equally aware with the advent of the embryonic shop that the situation remained the same, it was merely that the target had become more permanent. Thieves knew now where to find the valuable property which they sought to steal, they no longer needed to lie in wait in the forest hoping to observe and attack bands of itinerant merchants with their baggage trains, since by now the merchants had ceased to be nomadic, and were leading a settled existence.

The process of translation, whereby fairs became markets with stalls, which became covered markets or permanent shops, took time, and it was never complete. There are still covered markets and for that matter fairs, as well as thousands of open market stalls. Judging by contemporary legislation, it seems highly likely that before and during this transition shop theft was rife. The harsh lessons learnt in the market-place were not forgotten when it came to constructing and using permanent shop-houses. For example, the same conventions relating to the 'counter' or boundary between customer and shopkeeper were still observed, unlike shops in other cultures where buyer and seller sit and talk in comfort in the back of the shop before bargaining with each other. From the shopkeeper's point of view, the customer was the source of his livelihood, and also, at the same time, an object of suspicion. The shop was organised around its stock and the protection of it. Only if the necessary security from robbery and theft could be obtained could business proceed at all.

In medieval times the businessmen who were most alert to theft were of course those who had most to lose, that is the jewellers, the goldsmiths and the silversmiths, who always kept their most valuable wares concealed from the view of the ordinary shopper to make it harder for the impromptu thief. This precious stone and metal shops' tradition of having a high degree of anxiety about theft, and awareness of it as a probable daily occurrence, is still maintained in modern jewellery shops. Such (justified) apprehension about theft has always meant that jewellers and the like have been quick to take advantage of any new security devices which have become available, from early iron bars on shop windows and heavy iron-studded oak doors to modern photo-electric alarm systems and radar sentries.[2]

The earliest shops and stalls of course had no glass windows, and this made it very easy for people to steal by just reaching in and grabbing articles. The invention of plate glass, enabling large sheets of it to be used for shop windows, must have done much to reduce opportunities for the thief. Cast plate glass, in its earliest form, was invented in France in 1688, the Huguenots introducing it into England in 1773. Prior to the widespread use of plate glass for shop windows (which was not until the twentieth century) large shop windows were built up by using either leaded lights – that is, small panes of clear glass set in lead frames – or by using larger panes of obscured 'bull's-eye' glass set in wooden frames.³

Gradually, over the years, the permanent shop established itself as a separate institution. Its heyday was the nineteenth century, when the aim of the existing shops was to become paragons of precise orderliness and respectability. At this time, it must be remembered, most food was still sold in markets, and proper purpose-built shops were, outside urban areas, a rarity, existing to supply consumer durables and textiles. Davis says (1966, p. 253): 'The importance of markets little over a hundred years ago can perhaps best be realised by the fact that to-day over half the shops in Great Britain are food-shops, while at that time most of the food sold passed through the markets.'

The large, urban, nineteenth-century shop was not surprisingly a place where nineteenth-century virtues were well in evidence. Such shops were usually owned by one man, and they were clean, efficient, rational and made a profit. They reflected the beliefs of their best customers, and as such they were solid, sober, trading places which did not believe in lavishness or display and did not greatly value advertising. They tended to place their faith in selling quality goods from stark boards with good service from respectful shop assistants. Shops like these tried to build up a respectable clientele, and they tried to avoid selling to what were then known as 'the lower social orders', or for that matter even having such people on the premises. In terms of the prevailing morality then it was expected that most of the population would steal if given the chance and the aim of the shopkeeper was not to give that chance, and to achieve this through adequately 'policing' their shops to keep out the unwelcome and the unruly, and not to allow ordinary customers to be in the shop without an assistant at their elbow. The smaller urban shops, which modelled themselves on large stores, obviously had a greater theft problem since they were not able to be so exclusive with regard to customers, and their awareness of theft must have been correspondingly higher.

Department stores came into being from about 1875 onwards, catering for the needs of the middle and upper classes.⁴ The intention with department stores was that a shopper should be able to satisfy all his wants under one roof, in one shop which was divided into different departments, each of which was like a separate shop selling a different good. As it happens, at the end of the nineteenth century most department stores started from ordinary but successful clothing or drapery shops, and they grew by adding departments as their funds permitted. The 1971 Census of Distribution now defines department stores as shops with 25 or more persons engaged, selling a wide range of commodities including significant amounts of clothing and household goods. They must also have sales amounting to at least £15,000 per year, or at least 2 per cent of total annual turnover in each of five or more of the following commodity groups: (1) men's and boys' wear, (2) women's, girls' and children's wear, (3) footwear, (4) furniture and floor coverings, (5) radio, electrical and hardware, (6) food, (7) haberdashery and other drapery goods, (8) household textiles and soft furnishings, (9) miscellaneous. Finally, they must include at least one commodity group in each of the categories (1)–(3), (4)–(5), and (6)–(9).[5] In other words, then as now, such shops were enormous multi-purpose affairs requiring considerable capital to run and operate. Except in large urban areas, up until the end of the Second World War department stores were few in number for obvious reasons, since a fairly large catchment area of customers is required to support them.

None of the shops in existence in England throughout the nineteenth century were able to disregard the problem of theft, and each shop was organised in an attempt to minimise it. The result was that at the end of the century the shop, whether a corner store in a slum area, or a massive department store, had developed as a more or less perfect adaptation to combat theft. Apart from the structural and architectural ways in which this was achieved, control of theft was done mainly through prohibiting certain types of people from entering (larger shops would employ doormen for this purpose, smaller shops would use notices saying that certain categories of people would not be served), and by constantly waiting on customers with undivided attention.

Any change in this carefully calculated equilibrium occurring inside the shop could spell disaster in terms of allowing theft to occur, as many a shopkeeper bold enough to ignore the voice of experience and to try novel selling experiments could testify. To run a shop required a vast amount of accumulated wisdom and experience, and the lore of store-owning was not teachable. It had to be learnt the hard way, through costly mistakes. Not surprisingly, nineteenth-century shop-owners were markedly conservative in their outlook, and very wary of change for change's sake. The nineteenth-century shop had reached a pinnacle of development and perfection with regard both to selling and to controlling shop theft.

Very little substantive change in the shape, structure and selling techniques adopted by shops occurred from then on to the end of the Second World War. Such change as did occur was chiefly in the variety and appearance of the goods, and how they were prepared for sale (for example, tinning and pre-packaging became increasingly popular for all goods). Jefferys (1973) points out that from the end of the Second World War onwards there were suddenly introduced new forms of shop organisation, which changed the stable equilibrium that shops had arrived at. The most significant changes in shop organisation were the introduction of voluntary wholesale chains and retail buying groups, and new merchandising techniques, especially important being self-service and self-selection.[6] Self-service was first developed in America as a sales technique and its proposed introduction into England was initially regarded with scorn and horror by established, experienced, shop managers. Their view was that at the cost of a great deal of time, effort and ingenuity, they had finally reduced the theft problem to manageable proportions, and now the suggestion was that after all this customers should be allowed to help themselves! This would set at nought all the practical lessons of selling which had been so hardly won.

In 1950 there were less than 500 self-service grocery shops in England, ten years later there were 6,500. Despite all the adverse criticism and the comments that the idea of self-service had attracted, there were compelling reasons for accepting it ultimately in many retail areas. Customers liked it for a start, but the main pressure to change to self-service was the growing cost of shop labour. In the nineteenth century, as Davis (1966) makes clear, shop assistants usually lived in, and were prepared to work long hours for little pay, usually starting the day's work at 6 a.m. This picture was slowly changing, shop assistants now wanted higher wages. An important factor permitting the increase of self-service shops was better food packaging, which made possible long-term store of all retail items in convenient handlable units. (Breaking bulk had been the chief retail problem in the nineteenth century, long-term store facilities was the principal one in the twentieth century, solved principally by refrigeration.)

With the self-service shop, merchandise is displayed for the customer to see, touch and buy, without the intervention of sales staff.[7] Those shopkeepers who had objected to it on principal finally found that they were forced to become involved in it or fail in commercial competition. Self-service has various advantages for the customer and Fiber (1972, p. 187) gives a list of these. Under self-service, he says, the products can be seen and handled; there is less obligation to buy; all the articles are priced; the display is usually better and the service often quicker; and self-service suggests a progressive retailer, so that the customer is more likely to obtain what she wants and value for money.

Today's customer has indeed become used to self-service. However, it is easy to criticise Fiber's checklist. For example, it is not true that with counter-service shops goods cannot be seen or handled. They can be both seen and handled, but only with the help of a shop assistant. Further, with self-service, service is substantially non-existent, and to that extent only is it quicker than in counter-service shops. More to the point, Fiber also states on the same page: 'Self-service and to a lesser extent self-selection provide more opportunities for theft; losses tend to increase when either is first adopted.'

Jefferys (1973, p. 564) says that from 1945 onwards the retailer's aim is to make the merchandise sell itself. He argues that this trend had arisen as a result of wage increases in retailing, pointing out that previously at least two-thirds of an assistant's time in the shop was not spent selling at all, but was used up in arranging stock, waiting for customers and so on. Built-in selling, which is replacing human selling according to Jefferys, is achieved through heavy investment in advertising, packaging and labelling of the goods and through shopfitting and lighting. The aim of the technique is to increase manpower productivity in retailing by making its operation more continuous through greater use of capital. Fiber (1972, p. 97) agrees with this, saying: 'Retailing is becoming more mechanized to reduce running costs, though this involves higher initial capital investment.'

As soon as the self-service movement began in the 1950s it rapidly gathered momentum and spread quickly, since goods could be sold far more cheaply this way. More and more shopkeepers changed to self-service in order to avoid being undercut by their competitors. Shopkeepers also found that since far less staff were involved there was a substantial saving in wages. This saving meant that larger shop premises could be run quite economically under self-service. As staff dwindled, so shop size expanded. The logical conclusion was the emergence of the supermarket. A subsequent development to this, involving usually slightly less staff even than in a supermarket, is the discount house, where goods are for sale cheaper than elsewhere, because of economies effected on display and presentation. In the discount house goods are just left in boxes on shelves in what is effectively a warehouse atmosphere, and customers help themselves, paying at the checkout desk. In terms of appearance this really represents a reversion to the grim functionalism of the nineteenth-century shop, where no attempt is made as in the department store to create a pleasant purchasing atmosphere through skilful display; instead everything is being done to cut staffing bills, it being possible at the same time to keep retail prices low.

All of this of course, the development of self-service retail outlets especially, has completely turned over like an antheap the delicately established equilibrium obtaining in the nineteenth-century shop, and in relation to the control of theft many of the early lessons which the nineteenth-century shop embodied within it have been forgotten or ignored in the process. The implications in relation to shoplifting are fairly clear-cut.

Changes in shop type over time

Up until the end of the Second World War the commonest shop was small in size. The vast majority of people shopped in small, local, specialist shops, none of which were self-service. Now there have been marked changes in numbers and types of shops. Table 1 gives an indication of the general picture, showing changes in the number of retail shops over time.

Since 1950 the shops that have increased in number are multiples (chain stores with ten or more branches), off-licences, household good shops, shops selling furniture, radio and electrical goods (such as television sets) and hardware shops selling do-it-yourself goods, shops selling jewellery, leather and sports goods shops, general stores, and particularly department stores. In broad terms, this represents a growth in luxury goods shops on the one hand, and a tendency to increase scale on the other, to move in the direction of

Table 1 Number of retail establishments (Great Britain)

Type of shop	1950	1961	1971
Total retail shops	583,132	542,301	472,991
Co-operative societies	25,544	29,396	15,413
Multiples	53,949	66,701	66,785
Independents	503,639	446,204	390,793
Grocers and provision dealers	145,709	146,777	105,283
Other food retailers	137,867	114,655	92,524
Dairymen	10,231	6,573	3,853
Butchers	41,799	42,419	33,939
Fishmongers, poulterers	9,511	6,330	4,678
Greengrocers, fruiterers	43,948	33,073	23,318
Bread and flour confectioners	24,181	17,260	17,299
Off-licences	8,197	9,000	9,437
Confectioners, tobacconists, newsagents	74,606	70,108	52,064
Clothing and footwear shops	100,011	86,555	81,279
Footwear shops	14,870	14,104	13,445
Men's and boys' wear shops	15,581	13,577	14,619
Women's and girls' wear etc.	69,560	58,874	53,215
Household goods shops	54,081	60,343	70,342
Furniture and allied shops	16,104	16,498	22,131
Radio and electrical goods	11,761	16,517	17,942
Radio and TV hire shops	168	2,225	3,808
Hardware, china, wallpaper, paint	26,048	25,103	26,461
Other non-food retailers	69,217	60,113	66,724
Bookshops and stationers	10,388	5,967	6,001
Chemists, photographic dealers	18,205	18,097	16,670
Cycle and pram shops	8,865	5,630	2,793
Jewellery, leather and sports	18,896	17,506	21,786
Other non-food shops	12,863	12,913	19,474
General stores	1,641	3,750	4,775
Department stores	529	784	818
Variety and other general stores	1,112	2,966	3,957
Market stalls and mobile shops	—	35,006	31,790

SOURCE: Adapted from *Annual Abstract of Statistics* (1975) table 294, pp. 273–4.

more chain stores, and large multi-department shops. This has come about largely because of two factors, profitability of investment, and the growing cost of shop labour.

The concomitant diminution in the number of small shops has arisen mainly because of competition from larger enterprises with firmer financial backing and more capital, and partly because of the changed structure of taxing and overheads, all of which have operated against the small shop with its limited capital. This has meant a reduced number of small shops such as specialist food shops (for example, dairies, butchers, fishmongers, greengrocers, bakers and confectioners), and a reduction in the number of tobacconists, newsagents, bookshops, chemists and independent (non-chain) clothes shops. The functions of these shops have been mainly taken over by department stores, supermarkets and chain stores. Davis says (1966, p. 286): 'There is a tendency nowadays, widespread even among independent shopkeepers to think of themselves as general businessmen, rather than as specialist traders and it is especially noticeable in the food trades.'

There *are* still thousands of small shops, but to survive they must not be operating in competition with larger combines. The continued existence of small shops in high numbers seems problematic. This would imply that if shoplifting is easier in larger shops, or if it is easier in self-service shops (where there are less assistants), then we can logically expect the obvious: that rates of shoplifting will not be inhibited by current and expected shop type, or, more forcefully, that shoplifting figures can be expected to increase.

In the prevailing economic climate the small, counter-service shop cannot be expected to survive for long as a shop form, except in rural areas. An increase in the numbers of large supermarkets and the like can be predicted, since broadly such shops represent the optimum trading post for the modern shop-owner, for the reasons given above, if the shop-owner can afford to buy and run such shops initially. Only coincidentally do they also probably represent the optimum target from the point of view of the shoplifter.

At the opposite extreme are the most modern forms of shops, which have emerged relatively recently in Western Europe, such as supermarkets and department stores. The modern department store for example has particularly broken away from ideas of stark functionalism in design. It is a place where the shopper can linger, and probably wants to. In terms of space and warmth it is considerably warmer and larger than the private houses of most of the people who shop or work there, and as such it is inviting, and comfortable and pleasurable just to wander around in. This effect is enhanced by the department store as a visual spectacle, where experts in display and window-dressing have wrought special tableaux of luxury and stylish living, and have made the conventional and the commonplace seem somehow special, exciting, and desirable. In the modern department store the customer is encouraged to explore alone the Aladdin's caverns of modern wealth, and is constantly stimulated and challenged by the goods he sees, as he is confronted with yet more glittering, enticing display stands. More than that, the shop itself invites him to buy, reminding him of what he wants if he has forgotten, or what he *ought* to buy (irrespective of whether he can afford it), by printed statements exhorting him to make certain purchases, and sometimes by microphone announcements doing the same thing.[8]

The modern shop such as this quite frequently represents an example of stimulus overkill, where so many stimuli are crowded into each part of the shop that it is sometimes difficult for customers to find what they *do* really want in the welter of coloured posters, bright lights and labels.[9]

The development of such shops has partly been made possible by the advance of printing technology and electric techniques, particularly lighting, which offer to the shopkeeper ways of stimulating the customer which are novel and penetrating. Such shops have also come about as a result of past economic success, particularly postwar success, which produced a larger quantity of consumer goods, in turn demanding more retail outlets, and better, faster, more efficient ones. This has meant that since 1945 many more types of shops, particularly new specialist ones, have come into being, reflecting invention (such as shops selling metal alloy, plastic and rubber goods, and electrical and electronic products), and changes in customary behaviour (such as the rise of do-it-yourself shops to cater for the 'D.I.Y.' habit necessitated by the vast costs of professional labour), as well as the general availability of more luxury goods and their sale in specialist fancy goods shops.

Today's country shop and shops in underdeveloped countries still retain vestigial post-medieval functionalism, the shop being littered with piles of grimy, mundane, monochrome necessities, rather than multi-coloured displays of luxuries. Numbers of these shops dwindle rapidly in the face of more economical selling techniques involving different shop design.

The role of the shop assistant

In the shop the first line of defence against the shoplifter is the shop assistant, whether the shop is a department store, a supermarket, or a run-down village general store. Unfortunately the assistant is becoming relatively more and more expensive, due to increases in wages since the Second World War, and to cope with this, as was mentioned above, the trend in the distributive trades has been to try and find ways to distribute using just the bare minimum of staff. The tendency in the past was for shops to be labour intensive, for there to be nearly one assistant for each customer.[10] Nowadays a shopkeeper running his shop in this way would have such a large wage bill that he could scarcely afford to operate at all.

There is a tendency to economise on staff, and to try to reduce their number to the minimum through using self-service and self-selection techniques, where it is hoped that the goods will sell themselves without needing a small army of staff to do this work. The use of vending machines represents the logical conclusion of this sales policy, whereby not only are no assistants required at all, but also the customer can purchase at any time, since vending machines never close in the same way that shops do. All that is required is someone to collect the money, restock the machines with goods and change, and carry out periodic maintenance.

At present only a tiny handful of such fully automated shops exist in the centre of large urban areas, selling a restricted range of goods, chiefly foodstuffs. Most shops still have assistants, although in much reduced numbers in comparison with pre-war figures. It is the assistants rather than the shopkeeper who see the shoplifter in action and catch him, or at the worst it is the assistants who do not see the shoplifter and allow him to escape. Correspondingly, it becomes important to consider in a little more detail what kind of protection is afforded by shop assistants against shoplifting.

In large shops, for long periods during the day the shop assistant is relatively idle. This of course is not true of small shops. But in shops such as large department stores it is especially true in the early morning, before customers start to flock in. During these times of waiting there are of course tasks that have to be performed such as restocking shelves, labelling goods, dusting displays and so on, but much of the time may be spent in day-dreaming leaning on the counter, or in talking with other assistants. When there are slack times assistants will frequently try and make excuses to visit friends who are often located in different departments, and much time may be spent with them, amongst other things, enjoying the novelty and interest of being temporarily in a different environment, away from responsibilities.

At lunch-time such day-dreaming and 'visiting' is not possible, as the shop fills with customers asking questions and making purchases. At this time the assistant has to move swiftly, and may be very rushed, becoming as a result tired and irritable. Later in the afternoon the flow of customers diminishes, and finally there is a brief burst of renewed activity just before closing time. The precise pattern of the day varies a great deal from shop to shop, but in most shops there is a tendency for extremes to occur, that is for the assistants to be busy or idle as a result of the irregular flow of customers, which varies depending on such things as weather conditions or transport arrangements. This irregularity unquestionably creates different forms of unawareness throughout the day on the part of the shop assistant. At times of bustle and pressure the assistant is too busy to notice people and faces, and just registers the request and the money held out in the extended hand, and as she fumbles with wrapping papers and merchandise and change is too pressurised to examine the customer closely, and incapable of looking around to see what other customers are doing.

Lack of awareness as a result of day-dreaming occurs when the assistant has performed the necessary duties of rearranging goods and so forth, and becomes conscious of time hanging heavy on her hands. Gradually she finds there is nothing more that needs doing immediately, and as nothing happens she starts to dream, to mull over past events and to redigest them emotionally as well as imagining future ones. The tendency to day-dream may be increased by sheer physical tiredness as a result of standing up for long hours. The shop slowly recedes from her consciousness, and she becomes only dimly aware of the slow trickle of preoccupied customers moving apparently leisurely around the display stands. Infrequently and reluctantly the shop-girl has to abandon her reverie to answer some query, but she will return to it as soon as she can. This state of semi-sleep can be quickly broken if there is a rush of customers, but throughout the rest of the day the slow, languid movements of thoughtful shoppers, moving in an apparently aimless way, function in an almost hypnotic fashion. At such a time it is only quick, unusual movements or sharp commands or requests which will catch her attention, and start to get her involved again in the business of the shop.[11]

This implies that in large shops, for different reasons, there are quite long periods during the day when staff would be unlikely to notice shoplifters, unless the shoplifting is in some way striking. In so far as shoplifters are aware of the patterns of activity in a shop, aware for example that sharp, sudden movements are more likely to catch the eye than smooth, gradual ones, then it is even less likely that they will be noticed.

The same problems do not arise in the smaller shop, where it is unlikely that the owner or his assistants will ever have long periods of leisure to day-dream in. With less staff on the floor, the few assistants who are available will be kept busy throughout the day usually, restocking and rearranging. There will nearly always be work for them to do which will preclude them from falling into 'reverie-plus'.[12] Such shops are, however, just as vulnerable to shoplifters at peak times as larger stores. When for example on a Sunday morning, at about eleven a.m., the small newsagent's is just a 'sea of heads', then again the shopkeeper or his assistant will be much too busy to notice adroit thieves. Any thieves who are noticed are likely to be those engaging in an uncommon form of shoplifting in an uncommon way.

Reverting to larger stores, the 'listless apathy' of the assistant in the off-peak times makes it very easy for shoplifters (apart from the points mentioned below in the section on the social organisation of the shopping custom), who would probably tend to concentrate their activities in such larger stores anyway in preference to the smaller, counter-service store with the more alert (and self-interested) assistants. In the smaller shop, assistants and owners work together closely as a team, and anyone serving can appreciate that shoplifting can directly injure the business and both wages and profits. Correspondingly they are less likely to take a fatalistic attitude to it, arguing that it 'always occurs', and they are much more likely to be on the look-out for it. In large shops, because of the gulf between the manager and his assistants, it is not so clear to the assistants that shoplifting can directly affect them, and indeed it would take a longer time to do so in all probability. Usually assistants in such shops do not see themselves as involved at all in the business of the shop, and would always see moving to another shop as an alternative, should the one they work in go bankrupt for any reason. It is far too broad and facile a generalisation to say that they are alienated. It is simpler and more correct to say that they could not care less, that they are uninterested. In large shops the existence of security staff is likely to exacerbate this, since assistants can argue that the aspect of their role which is concerned with security has been removed from them, so why not leave it to the experts completely? It is also true that the larger self-service shop will see more shoplifting, and in turn assistants can become more blasé about it, arguing that it is so widespread that it is impossible to stop it, or else that the shop can afford it.

It is important to recall that people in large shops are *generally* less likely to be involved in their work than are people working in small enterprises. They are likely to know less about shop policy and finances, and to be hardly ever asked for advice. They are not involved, not especially wanted as individuals, it is merely their labour which is required, and even that is replaceable. Their value as persons, or the fact that as people they need to *be* valued, to have a sufficient level of self-esteem, is ignored. In the small organisation, in contrast, assistants are involved in the work of the shop, can see that they are needed and respected as individuals making a valuable contribution to the work of the enterprise, and do not suffer to the same degree from a felt sense of isolation and loneliness. Differential shoplifting rates between the two extremes of shop, the small and the large, are only a part of this. Inasmuch as the supermarket assistant is only marginally participating in the running of the business, it would not be at all surprising if she were only marginally interested in hampering the activities of shoplifters. The assistant from the small shop, however, will quite frequently stay on working late for a few minutes after the shop has shut to 'help out'. She is also almost certainly consulted from time to time by the owner of the shop as to her opinion on various matters, and is recognised as being a crucial part of the whole business, on a personality basis, rather than on a replaceable labour basis. This being the case, when she becomes aware of shoplifting she is more likely to try and do something to prevent it than is her opposite number working in the supermarket.

Out of this there gradually emerges the realisation that department stores and supermarkets (irrespective of their drawing powers for shoplifters) are more likely, without necessarily realising it, to tolerate and accept shoplifting, partly because it is harder to locate losses because of the amount of stock held, but particularly because of the role of the staff as very small replaceable cogs in large organisations which already have security staff, and which (with a few exceptions) usually make little attempt to involve the assistant in any way in the running of the shop, apart from the bare minimum. On top of this, as a separate issue, such large shops act like a magnet for the shoplifter, whether he be 'seedy, needy, or greedy', just because there is more there to be stolen, and it is apparently less closely checked and supervised. The sheer quantity of goods visible available for sale in the large shop makes it easier for the shoplifter to rationalise his actions in various ways too. For example, it might allow him to sustain dated prejudices relating to class hatred, because of the supposed wealth of those people who run large shops, so that he can argue that 'they can afford to lose a little', all of which can function as an additional impetus to steal.

In large department stores and supermarkets shoplifting can occur for hundreds of separate reasons, and can be seen as illustrating selfishness, human greed, or virtually anything else along similar lines, but to the shop manager the most important aspect of this is not shoplifting alone, but the final rate of 'shrinkage'. Shrinkage as a term represents total stock-loss, and it includes stock lost through damage or decay, as well as through theft, by delivery-men, shop staff, and shoplifting by customers. The implications of how the shrinkage figure is derived and the manifold motivations that may lie behind it are of less interest than what the total figure is.

If the figure is low in percentage terms in relation to turnover, then the profit curve will climb above it effortlessly on the graph, and the manager can then disregard shrinkage (including shoplifting). Such a stark, factual, economic approach is, in terms of prevailing morality, clearly a reprehensible stand to take given the issues at stake.

Self-evidently it is not the case that all managers are thinking in such limited terms about the distance between the profit curve and the shrinkage curve on the turnover graph (indeed many of them may not even know exactly how they stand in relation to shrinkage at all anyway). However, the managers who *are* thinking in curve terms alone are going to mentally write off shoplifting as part of shrinkage (in the same way that they write off other imponderables), whilst reserving the right to become outraged at any particular instance of it which persists in standing out from the background as a result of its flagrant or baroque nature. Such people are then likely to be among the first to argue that they ought to have greater protection via external control agencies, such as the police, from the depredations of shoplifters, having at this stage forgotten the simple logic of their own accounting approach to shrinkage, which is ignoring the morality involved in specific items, and concentrating instead only on the round number of thefts against the round amount of profit.

It is indeed interesting to consider how such shop managers are able to combine their initial moral indifference to the problem of shoplifting with the moral indignation which they display when it starts to present itself in a fashion which cannot be ignored, and how they manage to resolve this psychologically. I return to this issue in Chapter 4.

The social significance of the shopping custom

Good basic information on shopping practices is available in Adburgham (1964), Bradley and Fenwick (1975) and Davis (1966). Engel (1968, p. 437) begins a discussion of what he calls the purchasing process by stating a truism.

> Purchasing-process behaviour can be precipitated by two classes of variables. First, it can be problem oriented in the sense that the consumer visits a retail outlet in order to purchase a product or service that satisfies some perceived problem. In other words, problem recognition is one initiator of purchasing processes.
>
> All purchasing-process behaviour is certainly not problem-oriented, however. Visiting retail stores is often precipitated by other factors, including for example, a desire to get out of the house, a desire to get away from the spouse and children, a desire to avoid something unpleasant, or a desire to engage in fantasy.

Mair (1976) regards shopping in far broader terms as an activity, an economic unit of discourse and a relationship at one and the same time. He reviews the possible meanings of shopping for the consumer, emphasising especially the social component. Many housewives use 'a trip to the shops', as an escape from the home, and a chance to gossip with friends and make new acquaintances. Perhaps it is largely for this reason, the social aspect of shopping, that many house-bound wives and elderly people shop more than once a week, many in fact 'shopping' most days of the week, purchasing fairly small quantities on each occasion. To some extent this may be necessary for financial and other reasons too, of course (only the very rich can afford to buy in bulk at infrequent intervals), such as when the pension is paid for example, but it is unlikely to be due solely to bad organisation!

For the isolated and the lonely, invalids and the old, shopping is one of the very few social events. Males of course, who are caught up in the normal world of the adult employed with many more opportunities for socialising, and without the need to make the escape from the home as a semi-claustrophobic centre for routinised drudgery, will understandably see shopping in a completely different way, usually just as a means of purchasing and renewing scarce resources or perishables.

But for those not involved with employment, shopping remains the social event that it always has been. Shopping, as well as its obvious function, becomes an opportunity for fresh stimulation. Some shops can even become extensions of the home, female social centres, places where the tired, depressed and downtrodden can obtain temporary respite from their cares with others who live the same rigorous, weary, inexorable existence. For such people, to 'go shopping' means an opportunity to dress up for the occasion, to wear their best clothes, and to spend long minutes perhaps 'window-shopping' before finally buying amongst all the necessities a frivolous luxury item or two.

Shopping for many is a custom, if not a ritual, independent of its functional utility. Housewives, when they shop, may have special routes that they follow through the shopping area, moving from shop A to shop B, with particular shops having special personal meanings to them and serving social functions. Sometimes the shopping route is punctuated by a regular and ritualised 'break' taken in a tea-shop or café, something that the housewife always does when she goes out shopping and which has become a habit. This would imply that various types of shops and particular shops have special significance for the shopper.

Some shops may be characterised in a positive sense, as 'useful', 'honest', 'places where you can always get what you want', and 'helpful', and others may be seen in a negative sense as 'unhelpful', 'snobbish', 'places which never have what you want', or 'places where they never let you browse'. With small shops, such as corner grocery stores in areas of terraced housing, the shopper may know the shopkeeper as a friend or acquaintance and may sympathise with his troubles and struggles, knowing a lot about him personally, but the same is unlikely to be true of larger shops, just because of the selling pace and the greater quantity and faster turnover of assistants. Gradually over the years, as the housewife continues to shop in the same area, relationships of friendship and hostility with shopkeepers are developed and intensified which function to reinforce the idiosyncratic ritual of shopping, so that the shopper visits more frequently shops which she regards as being friendly and is likely to spend proportionately more time in these shops.

To a lesser extent, children's 'shopping' exhibits much the same patterning and inflexibility. There are for children especially favoured shops where the shopkeeper is a person who likes children and is not frightened of them, and there are hated shops where children are not encouraged to venture in, and will probably be asked to leave if they do. There are, too, a very few shops, such as sweet-shops, and toy and model shops, which are somehow invested with a special, semi-magical aura, where just being in the shop confers a feeling of well-being, wonder, contentment and euphoria on the child customer.

Only to those who are employed and busy are shops just functional warehouses which are not especially differentiated. To the rest of the population, housewives, children, the old and the isolated and the lonely, shops are much more than places to buy things quickly. Each shop has a special significance, and is used for special purposes on a ritualised basis, developed out of habit and experience. For such shoppers it is not just a question of finding a baker's shop, instead it is a question of going to a *particular* baker's shop, at a particular time, in a particular way, and in the process avoiding others, whether or not they have cheap offers or added inducements.

In this delicately elaborated world of the shopper reputations die hard, and shops acquire them quickly on the basis of facts, vague rumours, and little things such as small acts of courtesy, generosity or indifference made by shopkeepers. The tough, self-sufficient delicatessen owner can keep a filthy, unhygienic shop, but if he operates in areas of the country where toughness and self-sufficiency are valued, and seen as virtuous, then his shop is always likely to be crowded. To the individual 'social shopper', shopping is patterned in ways which are infinitely complex and local as well as being idiosyncratic. The amount of time shoppers will spend in different shops will vary accordingly; so will the way they address the assistants. This picture of extremely complex shopping activities is complicated still further by advertising and its effects, both on television and on billboards, and in the shop itself, which injects greater fluidity into the ritual of shopping in direct proportion to its success.

Viewed in these terms, it would be incorrect to think of shopping as direct purchase first and foremost, as advertising agencies are well aware. Certain shops attract disproportionate custom. It seems at the outset unlikely that shop theft can be regarded as occurring independently of this process. It would seem more likely that people are more prepared to steal from shops which they dislike (or else know nothing about) than from shops which they like, and still more prepared to steal from shops which present no *personal* image at all, such as supermarkets, where, as McClelland (1962) argues, the social aspect of shopping has been crushed out of existence.

If department stores and supermarkets are vulnerable to shoplifting generally, because of their impersonality and because of the tumescent, bulging affluence which their stocks suggest, making it easier for shoplifters to rationalise that they can afford loss, they are vulnerable in other ways too. Each ordinary counter-service shop which just sells one type of good has attached to it a different shoplifting risk. Some shops attract virtually no shoplifting, others may attract substantial theft, predominantly due to the type of merchandise which they are selling. The department store or supermarket, attempting to combine many shops in one, is attracting a high risk, because of its attempt to sell many different kinds of goods, the sale of each of which has a different type of risk linked to it.

Supermarkets and department stores have of course succeeded in drawing more customers than ordinary counter-service shops, and in selling more to more people. In turn they are larger on average than most specialist shops. It could be suggested that the very existence of such stores disturbs the delicate personal routine of the shopper's social shopping. Social shopping involves taking personal stances as to the worth of particular shops on the basis of the generated, evolving image of the shopkeeper (derived from gossip and hearsay), as the process of shopping continues over time. In the case of the department store and the supermarket, however, there is no image, nor, with a changing population of shop assistants, is it possible to construct one. The department store and the supermarket resist being categorised in personal terms at all, and instead only present a vision of a glittering paradise of acquirable, novel luxury. As such, these shops are outside the framework of sensitive judgements which constitutes the meaningful world of the social shopper.

It is possible to go even further, perhaps, and argue that in the case of supermarkets they are not seen as shops at all, since the service component, so long associated with shops, is almost entirely absent. The non-availability of any service minimises the transaction element, making it easier for customers to forget that there is a transaction taking place. Rather it appears as just a process of acquisitive collection, simply filling wire baskets and removing them to the safety and privacy of the car parked nearby. In counter-service shops there are constant reminders of the transaction. On first entering, customers are asked, 'Can I help you, sir?' implying a transaction about to take place, and throughout the process of purchasing there are further reminders that being in a shop is a two-way process, rather than orderly, slow-motion looting. This is achieved through, for example, statements about cheapness, bargain-value, better quality than is for sale elsewhere, made both verbally and personally.

From the point of view of the sales policy of supermarkets, there is everything to be said in favour of helping the customer to forget that there is a transaction taking place, since this way he will collect much more in his wire basket, and only at the end, near the checkout counter, realise that it is not free merely because it is disorganised, that he has to pay for it.[13]

The organisation of the shopping custom as described so far is the background against which the shoplifter works. The manifold complexities of interaction involved in shopping produce different kinds and types of shoppers, all of whom can, for example, provide valuable camouflage for the shoplifter. If all customers bought goods rationally and rapidly, without dawdling or meandering, it would then be much harder for the shoplifter to operate without detection. As it is, in any shopping area there is always a large volume of non-purchasing 'shoppers', people who just want to look and talk, as well as people shopping at different speeds and in different ways. In various shops there are various styles of appropriate shopping, people buy cheap items faster, more carelessly and more readily than they will buy expensive articles. All of this variation in buying, looking, and walking, even inside the shop, means that it becomes much more difficult for a shopkeeper to decide whether or not somebody is a potential thief waiting for his opportunity, or merely a careful purchaser who is making various mental decisions about the probable effect or result of his purchase while standing in front of the good.

The amount of redundant activity that surrounds most shopping offers usable cover for the shoplifter. The fact that most shoppers walk more than they need to, and look for longer than they need to, and in the process spend a great deal of time in the shop, is likely to make it much easier for a shoplifter to work, in that he can be more readily confused with *bona fide* shoppers. The sheer quantity of other shoppers in the area makes it easier for him to hide in the crowd once he has left the shop, and while in it, the physical presence of other shoppers makes it harder for assistants to observe the shoplifter in action if he takes care to use his cover carefully and stand close behind people, or at the right angle to them in relation to the assistant, or among large groups of them. The fact that these other, legitimate shoppers are preoccupied, or not expecting a shoplifter to 'have the nerve' to operate while they are there, means that he can get away with it if he is sufficiently vigilant and cautious. The post-Second World War invitation to shoppers to 'walk around without obligation' makes it very much easier for the shoplifter. Before this time it was never assumed that people entering a shop did not know what they wanted, or that they would leave without making a purchase, or would expect to be allowed to wander without supervision and intervention.

2

Shoplifting

The word 'shoplifting' is first heard of in England in the seventeenth century, in 1673.[1] Later, in 1680, Kirkman (Head and Kirkman, 1928) uses the word, saying, 'Towards Night these Houses are throng'd with People of all sorts . . . Shoplifters, Foilers, Bulkers.' The term 'shoplifting' was also used officially at this time. The preamble to the Act of Parliament 10 William III c. 12 (1698) states, 'The Crime of stealing Goods privately out of Shops and Warehouses [is] commonly called shoplifting.' From these references we can confidently state that the term 'shoplifting' dates from the seventeenth century, and that by the end of that century the word was well established in the English language. Contrary to popular supposition, the word was not recently coined to describe a recent phenomenon. The fact that the word has been in existence since the seventeenth century argues for the existence of the crime from this time onwards at least, although, as has been stated above, there is every reason to suppose that shoplifting has been in existence as a crime form as long as shops themselves.[2]

King William's Act decreed the death penalty for shoplifting, and it was to be 122 years before the punishment was even reduced to transportation for life. Romilly, the nineteenth-century self-appointed reformer of criminal law, set himself the task of attempting to change the law in relation to shoplifting in 1810, and support for the existing legislation was so strong that it was ten years before change occurred.[3] It is interesting to examine the steps that led to this, chronicled in the pages of Romilly's diary (Aspinall and Smith, 1959, pp. 391–3):

> *9 Feb. 1810.* Friday. I moved for and obtained leave to bring into the House of Commons three Bills, to repeal the Act of 10 & 11 Will. III c. 23, 12 Ann. st. 1 c. 7 and 24. Geo. II which punish with

death the crimes of stealing privately in a shop goods of the value of 5s. [25p], and of stealing to the amount of 40s. [£2], in dwelling houses, or on board vessels in navigable rivers. The Solicitor-General, with his usual panegyrics on the wisdom of past ages and declamations on the danger of interfering with what is already established, announced his intention of opposing the Bills after they should be brought in.

Sure enough, by May of the same year the Shoplifting Bill was rejected in the House of Lords. Romilly commented sadly, 'The argument principally relied on by those who spoke against the Bill was that innovations in criminal law were dangerous, and that the present measure was part of a system to innovate on the whole criminal code.'

In February 1811 he reintroduced his Shoplifting Bill into the House of Commons, and in May the Bill was rejected again by the Lords. But Romilly persisted, and introduced his Bill again into the Commons in January two years later. The diary continues:

> *26 March 1813.* The Bill to repeal the Act of King William making the offence of stealing privately in shops to the amount of 5s. a capital offence was read a third time in the Commons and passed. On the division, the numbers were, Ayes 72, Noes 34. . . .
> *2 April 1813.* The Bill was thrown out in the Lords to-day upon the second reading by a majority of 26 to 15. . . .
> *15 Feb. 1816.* The Bill to repeal the Shoplifting Act of King William was read a third time and passed. It would have passed, as it had done in all its former stages, without a word being said upon it, but I took this occasion to mention that while the Bill had been in its progress through the House, a boy of the name George Barrett, who was only ten years of age, had been convicted at the Old Bailey, under the Act, and was then lying in Newgate under sentence of death. I said that I should not have taken notice of the case of this miserable child if I had not observed that it was stated a little more than a year ago, in the newspapers, that the Recorder of London had declared, from the Bench at the Old Bailey, that 'it was the determination of the Prince Regent, in consequence of the number of boys who have been lately detected in committing felonies, to make an example of the next offender of this description who should be convicted, in order to give an effectual check to these numerous instances of depravity.'

What is clear from this is that shoplifting was feared in the seventeenth century, and that this fear had not much diminished by the nineteenth. The incisive and fiery Romilly succeeded in abolishing the death penalty for more than a hundred offences, but it was left to his follower, Sir James Mackintosh, to carry through in 1820 the Bill abolishing the death penalty for the offence of stealing 5s. from a shop.[4] For in that year poor Romilly, worn out with his efforts to break down obdurate resistance to reform, in despair committed suicide.

Years later in the nineteenth century, shoplifting, although differently and less harshly regarded, was still in existence as a crime form, but no longer punished by death. By the nineteenth century shoplifting was an art form involving complicated jargon, techniques and behaviours. Usually called theft rather than shoplifting, it was widespread and accepted as such.[5] This was the age when everything man-made had a value, and everything that had a value could be stolen for it. In those days handkerchieves, gloves and shirts were stolen from their surprised owners; it was the time when a man would even rush into a public house in order to steal a beer mug.[6] Anyone enterprising enough to start a shop could reasonably expect that others would be enterprising enough to try and steal from it. Perpetrators were treated as thieves, seen as a sub-set of the wider genus, members of the criminal classes, and they were punished with the same ruthless and indifferent rigidity as any other thieves.

The nineteenth-century shop represented the final stage in a long chain of evolution. Shops had evolved over time, becoming better and more efficient as experience suggested new ways of safe selling. Early experience showed that market barrows and stalls were more vulnerable than a 'shophouse' diligently overseen by the owner. The shop of the nineteenth century had evolved as the most efficient way of selling, combined with the least vulnerable layout of goods. The very fact that shops took the form that they did in the past in England indicates that the owners regarded theft as commonplace rather than extraordinary.

Writers on nineteenth-century criminal history such as Booth (1889–1902), and Mayhew (1861–2) document the intricacies of shop theft then, showing how professional, hierarchical and involved every aspect of underworld life then was. Chesney (1970, p. 155) has this to say:

As one might expect, stealing from shops was a crime at which women were outstanding, though it was not a feminine preserve. Indeed, then as now, it seems to have been a favourite game for a wide range of crooks. Circumstances, however, were different. Not only was more retailing done from stalls, but shopkeepers were much more given to displaying goods in the open.

Justices of the time were well aware of the effect of this practice in generating shop theft, as the following extract from *The Times* of the 1870s shows.

In the course of a case in which two boys were charged with stealing articles outside a shop in the Walworth Road, Mr. Ellison took occasion to comment on the temptation offered to thieves. During the twenty years he had been a magistrate, he and other magistrates had strongly condemned the practice. Tradesmen, however, still exposed their goods, owing to greed for gain. A tradesman in court said it was done in the ordinary course of business. Mr. Ellison said it was no excuse for such a practice which required to be checked.[7]

Chesney continues (1970, p. 155):

In poor districts, one often found narrow streets almost like oriental bazaars, lined with shops that were little more than open-fronted caves, their stock festooned about the entry or laid on trestles. These conditions encouraged street prowlers. Urchins, naturally [*sic*], were a particular bane to food sellers, who commonly thrashed out of hand those they caught. On foggy, twilit London evenings, gangs of youths would work their way through a poor shopping district, marking suitable plunder; then one lad would whip away a chosen object and disappear into the murk while others of the gang, idling in the road, acted as 'stalls' to obstruct and misdirect any pursuit.

Such gangs would of course be instantly turned out of better-class shops, had they tried to venture in, but it was a fairly common practice for a gang to cluster around a shop window, so that passers-by could not see what they were doing, and for one of them to quickly prise out one of the small panes of glass that made up the shop window, and thrust in his hand and steal whatever he could reach. The gang would then rapidly disperse. Such an operation would depend for its success upon speed and dexterity, and knowing this, shopkeepers must have been extremely wary of gangs of louts apparently aimlessly hanging around their shop fronts.

As far as can be ascertained there was a great deal of thieving in shops performed by adults. Male shoplifters were known to prefer jewellers' shops to other kinds because of the high unit value of each item. The usual technique was for a male shoplifter to pretend to be a legitimate but fussy customer, and to ask to see a range of rings and to appear indecisive about his choice, and request to see more until the counter was littered with jewellery. Then while chatting to the assistant he would wait his moment, perhaps even arranging for a confederate to make a carefully timed entry to distract the assistant, and stealthily and watchfully steal an article, express more indecision and slowly withdraw. Alternatively, such a shoplifter might have observed a ring in the jeweller's window some days in advance of his planned theft, and obtained or made a cheap replica of it. Then, upon entering the shop, he would ask to see the ring in question, and deftly substitute his own fake ring for it. Pocketing the real ring and returning the fake completes the theft known as 'ring-switching'.

Supposedly there were more female shoplifters than male, and such thieves would take virtually anything, employing truly amazing legerdemain and audacity. The pattern of taking was either opportunist, spur of the moment stealing of anything that was left unprotected even for an instant, or else planned theft with confederates who would enter the shop separately and pretend to be completely unconnected with the shoplifter. The confederate's job was twofold: to block the assistant's view of the shoplifter at the critical time of the theft, and to receive the stolen goods when they were slipped to her. With the latter type of premeditated shoplifting a woman might go into a shop and demand to see a quantity of goods, sufficient to get the overworked shopkeeper busy and flustered. She would, as with her male counterpart, put on an act of being a refined lady who was hard to please, and as soon as an opportunity presented itself would steal an item or two, small articles being preferred, and pass the goods to the confederate, who would leave the shop immediately.

The rigidity of social life then set fixed limits on what a thief could do, and where he could go without occasioning comment. A society with a rigid class system, where members of each class tried hard to look as different from each other as possible, and with shops which only catered for a fixed clientele drawn from one of these class groups, meant that shoplifters would usually be confined to working one type of shop in one particular way. Out of this there emerges the, to us, curious and dated hierarchies of criminals each operating in a fairly limited sector. To step outside this sector would require considerable acting skill in copying accent, gestures and demeanour of another group, and the slightest inaccuracy in portrayal would lead to immediate unmasking.

Shoplifting in the nineteenth century, along with all other crime, was extremely specialist, and criminals then did not display the flexible generalism which has become so common among modern law-breakers, who may hedge their bets through intermittent practice of a number of different forms of crime. What is so noticeable about this era is that the severity of the punishment then available seemed to have no effect on the level of shoplifting. Even children would steal from under a shopkeeper's nose, and if they were caught, at best they would receive a vicious beating from him, and at worst it would mean imprisonment or transportation. Yet both children and adults continued to steal, almost as if there were no punishment for it, indicating that even the most horrific of the nineteenth-century punishments had no deterrent value, except in the minds of the legislators.

Such was the picture in the past. Since then there have been extensive economic, cultural and legislative changes. The type and population of shops has changed, and so have the goods in them, and the customers who use them. Up until 1968 the Act of Parliament which regulated shoplifting was the Larceny Act of 1916, which set up a rather complicated set of categories of larceny. With the Theft Act of 1968 this was rationalised, and the whole legislation in relation to theft was simplified. Theft from now on is defined as dishonest appropriation of property belonging to another with the intention of permanently depriving the other of it. Attached to the offence of theft there is a maximum penalty of ten years' imprisonment. For the offence of handling stolen goods there is a maximum penalty of fourteen years' imprisonment. In the official Home Office list of indictable offences, Offence 46, Larceny from shops and stalls, is replaced by Shoplifting. However, changes in legislation and classification have *not* affected shoplifting as an offence.

Below in Table 2 are listed some annual averages and yearly figures of shoplifting offences known to the police.

Table 2 *Numbers of shoplifting offences known to the police (England and Wales)*

	Year	Number of offences
Annual average	1935–39	15,957
	1940–44	18,017
	1945–49	18,567
	1950–54	23,094
	1955–59	29,614
	1960–64	51,800
Yearly figures	1963	55,906
	1964	60,139
	1965	66,427
	1966	68,288
	1967	70,971
	1968	78,490
	1969	91,169
	1970	101,822
	1971	119,281
	1972	126,844
	1973	130,161
	1974	164,063
	1975	175,552
	1976	180,993

SOURCE: *Criminal Statistics (England and Wales)* (H.M.S.O.)

From the 1939 pre-war rate, offences have quadrupled to over 60,000 in 1964. The 1964 figure itself is more than doubled eight years later in 1972. We now have a more than eleven-fold increase in figures from the 1939 base. Some of this can perhaps be accounted for by differential reporting and awareness, but there remains a staggering increase in numbers of thefts to account for, particularly from the mid-1960s onwards, which can only and obviously indicate a vast increase in theft occurring independently of legislative changes.

Table 3 shows the area distribution of shoplifting offences for the

Table 3 Area distribution of shoplifting offences known to the police (England)

Police force area	Number of offences		
	1974	1975	1976
Avon and Somerset	3,094	4,635	4,464
Bedfordshire	1,432	2,145	2,201
Cambridgeshire	2,354	3,523	2,771
Cheshire	1,888	2,813	3,052
Cleveland	2,583	3,223	3,406
Cumbria	1,201	1,690	1,402
Derbyshire	1,770	2,477	2,771
Devon and Cornwall	2,980	4,022	3,805
Dorset	1,708	2,645	2,291
Durham	1,165	1,686	1,712
Essex	3,499	4,631	4,778
Gloucestershire	1,740	1,872	1,940
Greater Manchester	7,726	11,681	12,093
Hampshire	4,095	6,085	5,603
Hertfordshire	1,902	2,968	3,233
Humberside	2,286	3,249	3,622
Kent	2,732	4,109	4,439
Lancashire	3,450	4,412	4,512
Leicestershire	1,555	2,181	2,302
Lincolnshire	1,208	1,584	1,796
London, City of	90	108	138
Merseyside	5,126	6,946	6,486
Metropolitan Police District	15,311	23,501	24,599
Norfolk	1,552	2,174	2,060
Northamptonshire	1,002	1,552	1,930
Northumbria	4,237	6,389	6,980
North Yorkshire	1,605	1,822	2,613
Nottinghamshire	4,500	5,942	5,653
South Yorkshire	3,316	5,244	5,796
Staffordshire	2,481	2,706	2,910
Suffolk	1,556	2,003	2,071
Surrey	1,361	2,039	2,215
Sussex	4,518	5,943	6,077
Thames Valley	3,801	5,870	6,174
Warwickshire	811	1,093	1,158
West Mercia	1,843	2,176	2,270
West Midlands	6,413	9,011	9,907
West Yorkshire	5,681	8,794	8,693
Wiltshire	1,754	1,600	2,029
England	156,999	166,544	171,952
England and Wales	164,063	175,552	180,993

SOURCE: *Criminal Statistics (England and Wales)* (H.M.S.O.)

last three years, showing how the national total is broken up and distributed among the various constituent regions. The greatest concentrations of course are in urban areas, where there are also dense concentrations of shops offering availability and plenty of choice for the shoplifter.

The only possible conclusion that can be drawn from a brief perusal of this type of official information is that shoplifting as a crime form is on the increase in a very big way in this country. This prompts the next question: Are there any factors in existence now likely to inhibit the growing popularity of shoplifting as a criminal activity? Regrettably, few can be identified, unless and until commercial policies change to alter the structure of availability for the thief. At present one can only presume that rates are likely to increase, and this cannot be seen as a reflection on the police and their activity, since they are very much the servant of the public. Even if collectively, as a community, we were to ask them to change their priorities in relation to crime, we are still faced with hard economic facts. In the area of the study, Devon and Cornwall, the total size of the population is roughly 1,312,040 (1975 figures), with a police force to patrol this of less than 3,000 men and women.[8] Inevitably this means that certain types of crime must have poorer clear-up rates than others. As far as shoplifting is concerned, there is very little the police *can* do with this type of offence (except in terms of rarely heeded crime prevention advice), occurring as it does on semi-private, semi-public, secluded land, unless and until they are actually called in.

So we are faced with the rather alarming realisation that there are virtually no checks to this type of offence which can be expected to automatically cut in and constrain it. Shoplifting is a growth sector in the crime industry.

Nine questions for the shoplifter

With shoplifting it may be an unwarranted assumption to presume that the operations of the criminal are guided by rationality, apart from anything else because there are so many worlds of rationality. It certainly must be incorrect to assume that most shoplifters are irrational or mentally unstable. This type of myth merely functions to smooth the path for the on-the-street shoplifter.

Presuming for the moment that most shoplifters can foresee the consequences of their actions, and do know what they are doing, it may be instructive to consider the various problems that the shoplifter faces as he rapidly takes decisions about whether or not to steal from one particular shop (rather than another), trying to see things his way. Through so doing it may become clearer as to how to forestall this activity. Not every shoplifter will actually ask himself these particular questions in this particular form, nor may the activity be consciously decided upon, and further the mental processes involved will be extremely rapid.

In shoplifting, the potential criminal must first ask:
Is this a shop which contains things which I want?
That is, items for personal use, for resale or for gifts. In this assessment, clearly such shops as wholesalers and monumental masons are excluded. The potential shoplifter's next question must be:
Shall I take these things without paying?
It would be naïve to assume that people who shoplift invariably do so; there will be some shops that they do actually purchase goods from. It is probable, too, that these shops possess some special characteristics. All too little is known about the shops where the shoplifter does make legitimate purchases and why. (Possibly the owner is known, possibly it is too difficult to steal or perhaps certain types of goods, such as meat and vegetables, are rarely stolen by anybody.) It is at this stage that morality and motive enter the picture, and this is discussed more fully below. Before this, however, it might be instructive to consider some of the other questions which the potential shoplifter must ask himself.
Which articles shall I take?
Presuming that a decision to steal has been reached, and following on from this,
Can these things be taken easily?
The answer to this must lie in the answers to certain subsidiary questions, chiefly,
Are the goods on display and accessible?
If the goods are wrapped and neatly pre-packaged in cellophane, then they are easily removed, but if they are behind counters on shelves, or in drawers or large boxes, or in glass display cabinets, then removal is much more complicated. Frequently in modern shops the goods are apparently unprotected and readily available in order to facilitate impulse purchase. The next question for the shoplifter is,

Can the goods be easily concealed?
The form of the concealment can vary a great deal.[9] It might be adequate in some shops for the goods to be openly carried until the very last minute when the shoplifter passes through the final barrier before escaping to the street outside the shop, or again it might be judged necessary for the goods to be hidden on his person, or in a bag. The drawback to this, from the thief's point of view, is that if he is caught and searched on suspicion, if the goods have been obviously hidden he is less likely to be able to brazen his way out of the situation. Small, compact items are more likely to be favoured if direct concealment is necessary, and the higher the unit value of each the better. So wrist-watches, pocket-knives, pens, necklaces or brooches would be more at risk than bolts of cloth or other, larger, relatively low value items that are difficult to conceal. Next:
Will anyone be able to see the goods being concealed?
If direct hiding is necessary, then the thief will need suitable seclusion in which to do so. He must make an estimate of whether or not such 'cover' exists in the shop, areas which are blind spots for shop assistants' observation, such as behind display stands, or in alcoves or recesses in the shop. The act of concealment may take a moment or so, since as an extra precaution it may be necessary for the thief to strip off wrappings, or remove price labels and substitute others from another shop, so that if he *is* searched he will have a story ready, arguing that, for example, he bought the goods elsewhere, before he came into the shop.
Once the theft has occurred (or while it is occurring) can shop assistants be evaded?
If there are a large number of mobile, vigilant and attentive assistants, then it will be difficult for the thief to operate, but if, in his view, there are relatively few, inattentive assistants, then this would make it a much more attractive proposition.[10] Probably a time will be chosen when this criterion is more likely to be met, such as extremes of the day, or the busy lunch-time period. Now the potential shoplifter must ask,
Is there more than one escape route?
The main, most obvious route, is that which customers are expected to take, past the till, or the counter, and so out through the door. If, however, there are other routes, or a large number of different doors, then this is more likely to help the thief in making up his mind that theft is possible here. Due to fire regulations few shops do only

have one entrance and exit, and this would operate to the shoplifter's advantage, since all the exits cannot be watched with equal vigilance, particularly not when the shop is crowded with customers. The final decision that the potential shoplifter must take before deciding whether or not he will steal is to select an excuse for use if caught stealing. If in the middle of his activities he is interrupted by a store detective, it is imperative from his point of view that he is not easily identified as a shoplifter straightaway, or indeed at all. To counter recognition he will prepare to say that he was just going to pay for the goods, or that he intended to pay, or that he absent-mindedly had forgotten to pay, or that he was just taking the goods outside into the daylight so that he could see them more clearly, or that he had not in fact deliberately picked up the goods at all, that somehow they must have fallen into his bag by mistake, or that without realising it he had picked up two of the same object, and had paid for one without realising that he had the other, and so on. In the nature of things it may be very difficult for the shop staff to prove or disprove any of these statements. The thief is aware of this, and knows that if he produces a firm story fast, rather than dithering, then even if he is caught, the probability is that he will be released for lack of clear evidence.

If each of these questions can be answered satisfactorily from the thief's point of view, then stealing will occur, and it may or may not be detected. Without a great deal of difficulty there emerges a picture of the type of shop that is more likely to be stolen from, and the type of shop where shoplifting is virtually impossible, this arising from attempting to look at the shop and its contents from the point of view of the rational thief. I am not suggesting that any shoplifter will consciously pose for himself the kind of questions that have been listed above. The greater probability is that decisions concerning availability and opportunity will have to be taken, but that these will be taken extremely rapidly by the shoplifter, who will then move into action more or less immediately, but only if he perceives subjectively that shoplifting is possible without a great deal of effort or ingenuity. It is possible that his subjective assessment is technically wrong, that he has not noticed certain critical features of shop arrangement which will inevitably lead to his identification, capture and arrest, but the objective situation is less important than his appraisal of it.

For example, if there is in a shop a prominently displayed notice saying that closed-circuit television is in operation, the shoplifter may argue to himself that:

1. He can operate so swiftly that even when noticed he will have left the shop before he can be caught.
2. He can so camouflage his activities that the person monitoring the control screens will not be able to spot him at work.
3. Such notices are merely put there as a deterrent, and that no such system is in operation.
4. The screens are present as a deterrent, and the control system is unmanned.
5. The control system is operational and manned, but that the limited span of attention of an operator will work in favour of the thief.

(A further possibility exists, that the shoplifter may not have seen the notices.)

If one or more of these views are held by the shoplifter, then he will go ahead and steal, on the basis of his subjective assessment of the shop's defences. Let us suppose that CCTV is in operation, and that he is caught as a result. The shoplifter's behaviour may seem poorly planned and foolish from the operator's point of view, knowing what he does about the efficiency of the system, but the objectivity of the situation is much less important than the shoplifter's previous experience of similar systems and his subjective judgement.

It is very possible that shopkeepers are thinking less about the appearance of their shop from the shoplifter's point of view than they are about the level of police protection which they require from shoplifters (irrespective of its feasibility), and the extent to which customers *ought* to have a constraining morality which will prevent them from engaging in shoplifting, whether or not it is objectively or subjectively possible as an activity.

Motives for shoplifting

Much information has already been gathered on the motives that drive people to shoplift. See, for example, Cameron (1964), Gibbens (1962) and Belson (1969). I do not wish to go into a great deal of detail here about motive, partly because it has been covered so well elsewhere, and partly because of the aims of this study. It is however perhaps as well to review briefly some of the main alleged causes, motives and precipitating states that can produce shoplifting.

Precipitating mental states

In the past, up until the 1960s, it had always been assumed that there was a condition, known as kleptomania, which was responsible for most shoplifting.[11] Kleptomania was thought to be a compulsive disorder of the personality which exhibited itself in the form of continual shoplifting without reason. Dawson (1946, p. 235), has this to say about it: 'Some cases of so-called kleptomania are most difficult to judge, but where there occurs a persistent purloining of trivial articles in spite of punishment, mental deficiency or other abnormality should be suspected.' This quotation reveals the very confused and muddled state of psychiatry at this time, when large numbers of putative syndromes were supposedly isolated, and given names with Greek and Latin prefixes, and the rest was left to current prejudice. However, it has now been realised by psychiatrists that there is no such thing as kleptomania, and that there never has been, and that usually where continual stealing takes place it is easier to use an alternative explanation.

Some shoplifting can occur as a result of mental handicap, where the person has a level of intelligence below the normal, and simply cannot understand, far less follow, the mass of complex rules that most citizens habitually use.[12] Slater and Roth (1970, p. 716) make some interesting comments on the proneness of certain categories of the mentally handicapped to become involved in shoplifting:

> and feeble-minded children are sometimes used by parents for shoplifting and pilfering. Thefts in big stores and shops are a common offence, especially among girls, and appear to constitute a somewhat greater temptation for girls of dull intelligence. In the study by Cowie *et al.* (1968) of a year's intake into a girls' classifying school a significant excess of cases of larceny was found among the girls of IQ 70–9; but among the girls of IQ below 70, there were very few offenders and almost all the 'delinquency' was of a sexual nature.

Slater and Roth continue, referring to a different issue, the possibility that shoplifting or other crime is produced by mental disturbances arising from the female menstrual cycle, 'Practice in the Courts suggests that offences are more likely in girls during the premenstruum, one of the many phenomena associated with the increased state of emotional tension at that time. Katherina Dalton (1960) has demonstrated very elegantly the association in schoolgirls of misbehaviour with menstruation.' Shoplifting could also be caused by stress or fatigue, depression,[13] or perhaps through personality disorder,[14] but no such explanation would do more than describe a handful of cases. It certainly would not be a main precipitating factor for all those who shoplift.

Precipitating physical states

Some evidence does exist to show that some types of physical illness can cause a clouding of consciousness and confusion sufficient to cause various sorts of rule breaking. For example, the work done by Yoshimasu (1965) on the prodromal stage of Huntington's chorea, Stutt's work (1965) on diabetes mellitus in a state of hypoglycaemia, and Schipkovensky's study on cerebral arteriosclerosis (1965). Under certain circumstances these disease conditions may lead to crime, and within that possibly some shoplifting occurs as a direct result of a physical condition which temporarily or permanently does not allow the owner to distinguish right from wrong, but again the numbers of people involved must be slight.

Possibly more significant physical causes of shoplifting, apart from these special cases, are senility and pregnancy. Shoplifting occurs with the senile as a result of memory failure, and general confusion, whereas with pregnant women it may occur because of absent-mindedness, emotionality, and a sense of not having full capabilities due to hormonal changes. Both shopkeepers and the police are reputed to extend a good deal of sympathy and compassion to these two groups, with good reason, which makes it harder in a way to know what their contribution to shoplifting is, but there is every reason to suppose that it must be a sizeable fraction.

A third possible physical illness issue is one which I have discussed elsewhere (Walsh, 1969), the crux of the argument being that there may be a small section of the physically afflicted who, seeing themselves as stigmatised by the community, may elect not to abide by its rules, which they see as only relating to the physically normal. This again could result in a small quantity of recidivist shoplifting amongst other petty crime.

Generally, though, with physical as with mental states, it is not possible to see these as contributing significantly to shoplifting as a crime form, although the details may repay study. There is no reason to suppose that most shoplifters are mentally or physically ill, any more than there is to suppose that most criminals in general are so afflicted, although, of course, after detection, some shoplifters may plead that before the crime they had a more or less pertinent physical or mental disorder at the time.

The poverty motive

Much has been made of the poverty motive in the past for all crime, including shoplifting. It has been argued that people in need are desperate, and that much shoplifting of food and other necessaries is done by such individuals. This may have been so in the past prior to the Second World War. Undeniably economic pressure does provide a motive for theft of all sorts, including shoplifting, and we cannot effortlessly gainsay this by talking in terms of social service provision. The young mother of a large family who cannot afford shoes for her children may feel tempted to steal them, and the existence of social services is not very likely to improve the position from her point of view.

However, the group who face most adverse economic pressure, the poorest in the land, are not by and large the young at all, but the old. If the poverty argument were true, then we should expect that thousands of old-age pensioners would stand accused of shoplifting. They do not. Assessment is complicated by the point made above, that many agencies who make decisions as to who is to be a shoplifter and who is not exercise considerable tolerance and latitude in dealing with the elderly, on the grounds that their eyesight is bad, that they can easily become confused by overstimulation, and that generally speaking allowances must be made for those with failing powers. This means that we never know exactly how many of the elderly do shoplift.

Rowntree's study (1902) made it quite clear that poverty is so very relative as a term. More or less anyone can be said to be in a state of poverty, depending upon their standards, their past experience and their expectations. What can be done to alleviate cases of greatest and most obvious hardship in this country is done. On this basis it appears highly improbable that most shoplifting is done because of poverty.

Youthfulness as a pressure

Youth itself can be a potent producer of shoplifting. The child can take great pleasure in testing out adults' skills, and in outwitting grown-ups. This can take the form of word games or mathematical puzzles put to the adult, to which the child already has the answer, or shoplifting, where the child's stealing is part of an exploration of adult capacity and morality, with an obvious exciting reward for its own skill in sleight of hand. Much of this childish shoplifting takes the form of a prank, and it may only be the sheer monetary worth of what is stolen which makes it appear otherwise. In the past when people observed children stealing apples from orchards, they said, 'boys will be boys'. Now that we have replaced our orchards with motorways and shopping precincts, children still take what they can reach, as they have always done, whether it is an apple or a plastic train. In the world of the child, gang pressure may function to force children to do what adults call stealing, and it is very often the case that one child will start to shoplift from idiosyncratic motives, and others will engage in emulative behaviour as a result of group pressure; not to do so would prejudice the chances of remaining accepted.

This kind of shoplifting occurs either because early socialisation has failed (or not been present in sufficient quantity, with sufficient impact), or else while it is still continuing.[15] Children cannot overnight absorb, assimilate and digest all the moral rules of a community. The process of absorption takes time, and there is a lag. While it continues, so does the shoplifting. The fact that a child shoplifts need not mean that he will always do so. This behaviour can perhaps best be seen as a passing phase in the child's moral development, usually regarded as more than that, because of the economic worth of what is there to take. Reverting to the apple example, the loss of a dozen apples is piffling to the owner of an orchard, but the loss of some expensive toys to a shop-owner may seem to be a much more serious affair, which it is of course. To the child the events are scarcely distinguishable, except in terms of marginal utility.

Greed as a motive

The most obvious motive for shoplifting is greed. In modern industrial societies people are under constant pressure to accept competitive, private, individual materialism as an ideology.[16] Advertising, for example, appears to remind and tell people that all forms of contentment and gratification are only possible through the acquisition of particular material goods. Ownership of a particular artefact is equated with happiness, pleasure and satisfaction. This materialist emphasis is intensified as customers are exhorted to buy, own and have, in a variety of ingenious and subtle ways. Boxes of chocolates are advertised by such moral imperatives as 'Go on! Spoil yourself! You deserve it!' Wrist-watches are advertised by statements such as 'Can you afford to be without it?' Perhaps an overall message is 'If you want it, you ought to have it,' not at some point in the future, but now, immediately, instantly.

At the same time as people are subjected to ever-increasing materialist emphases, they are also learning to have never-ending needs, needs for more and more goods. In a community which has produced a sizeable range of portable, personal luxuries, both consumable and permanent, how does the individual citizen know when he has acquired enough? Is he learning instead to want *everything* that is available, to constantly feel that he needs to acquire more?

Very probably we would have to say that greed *was* the most important motive for shoplifting (and also perhaps for shopkeeping). There are no clear limits to what an individual's wants should be, no definitions. Instead there is ever-increasing pressure for people to acquire and buy more and more, mechanically without thought. Faced with these rather absurd pressures, many people may find that they run short of spending money when they attempt to buy (not surprisingly). Some may decide to 'save' by shoplifting, or they may shoplift only luxuries, or they may spend all their money on luxuries (because these are more forcefully advertised to get them to sell at all), and feel that they have to shoplift to acquire necessities. Alternatively, the greed may be an isolated instance, rather than a continuing thing. None of this is very surprising, given the pressures the individual faces to see greed as a normal end-state, and not to be happy unless he is acquiring more and more, regardless of whether he needs it or not. This is a price that we must pay for sheer availability of goods, sad though it is.

'Ideological' motives

A further motive, of recent introduction, can be ideology. There are some thousands of people who genuinely believe that shoplifting is sensible and practical behaviour. The ideology that supports this is rooted in politics which are opposed to capitalism, in other words, communism. As a belief system this part of communism gained ground amongst some sections of the new middle class in England in the late 1960s. The essential argument is that capitalism and the established society are injurious, and built on exploitation (an extrapolation from Marx's ideas). Large shops and business companies are seen as representing the ill-gotten gains of the capitalist, and according to this belief these gains must be redistributed in some new way, preferably equitably.

Marx's writings made it clear that this redistribution would occur 'naturally' after the ultimate revolution which would usher in the Dictatorship of the Proletariat, but in the meantime adherents of these beliefs feel that theft and shoplifting represent means of destroying and overthrowing the established order faster, through literally wrecking capitalism, transaction by transaction.

For small quantities of such political believers shoplifting then serves two purposes: not only does it enable them to feel that through pursuing self-interest they are really being public-spirited, but also it gives them more commodities. In fact such beliefs provide the perfect rationalisation for theft. The idea that all shops are enormously wealthy is of course absurd, as absurd as thinking that such petty shoplifting will change the course of history and produce the revolution that Marx predicted.

Numerically, such a group of political missionaries does little to affect the shoplifting rate, but as with shoplifters who suffer from mental or physical illness, when caught, they receive disproportionate publicity, suggesting that such states are widespread.

The 'game' motive

Miller (1958) put forward the idea that excitement may be a goal in itself for many criminals. Shoplifting for many may well offer excitement, and be an exciting game, rather than an offence, as viewed from the offender's view point. Engaging in a forbidden act has various things attached to it, the reward accruing from the commission of the act (in this case, the worth of the stolen goods to the offender, rather than their monetary worth), the punishment accruing from the commission, and the excitement of committing the act, knowing it to be forbidden, together with further excitement arising from the uncertainty of the actual outcome. The offender does not know for sure, before he steals, whether or not he will be caught, and whether or not he can evade capture. The same thing applies in the children's game of 'blind man's buff', together with the same excitement.

Predatory shoplifting is a gamble, and it may also be thrilling for those who engage in it.[17] It may also be that, caught up in the excitement of trying to evade detection and capture, perpetrators forget the seriousness of what they are actually doing, and temporarily at least do not realise it. The 'game' of shoplifting from the offender's point of view consists in controlling the delirious excitement that he realises he will feel as he removes the tantalising object and escapes with it, and if he does outwit the shopkeeper and avoid capture, recollecting that excitement in tranquillity. For such people this type of shoplifting for excitement may be directly attractive in so far as they usually lead highly routinised existences which they find irksome and devoid of any real meaning or fresh stimulation. To actually be caught almost seems unfair, and the perpetrator is very frequently numb with shock on capture, when he realises the way in which this act will be regarded by other people. There are strong reasons for supposing that this process – the game motive – may contribute significantly to shoplifting, and not just in relation to children either. This may perhaps be partly because in a society which emphasises rationality and is usually threatened by apparent irrationality, games are frowned upon (unless highly ritualised, such as cricket and football), despite the 'fun-ethic'; thus alternative non-criminal games of a spontaneous type for young adults and adults, offering the same excitement, are extremely limited in number.[18]

This list of motives by no means exhausts the possible motives for shoplifting, which are myriad and various. Of course most of them could be subsumed under a general category of 'lack of morality', but this rather misses the very important point as to why shoplifting exists and is so widespread. It would also mean that such subsidiary questions as asking what are the conditions under which people are able to successfully neutralise their own morality, to use Matza's term (1964), are likely to be glossed over. One further motive needs comment, and that is shoplifting for a livelihood, in other words professional shoplifting for gain.

Professional shoplifters

Much mention is made of the professional shoplifter by shopkeepers and members of the public. It is said that the numbers of professionals is high and increasing. It is true that well-organised habitual shoplifters will steal more than occasional shoplifters. It is also true that because of this they are more likely to be caught sooner and put out of circulation earlier. Shopkeepers who perhaps are relatively indifferent to the loss of the occasional few small items will make a stand and engage in concerted action against organised bands of thieves, because the danger is so much more clearly apparent. Large stores faced with this may co-operate with each other, and arrange 'early warning' telephone systems designed to chart the movements of gangs in their area, and it is certainly much more likely that the police will be involved at an early stage to deal with this branch of crime, if indeed the impetus does not come from them in the first place, which is more likely.[19]

Professionals must rely heavily upon anonymity, which commits them to mobility and travel. This instantly denies them the advantage of local knowledge, which may operate to their detriment. Further, they are committed to restricting their operations to desirable targets, located largely in town centres, where awareness of, and opposition to, shoplifting is anyway likely to be greater, which again sets a definite limit to the 'life' of their operations.

The probability is that the term 'professional' is often misapplied to shoplifters. Apart from repetitious activity, the term implies skill, expertise and rational commitment. Professional shoplifting in this sense is a craft-crime, which has probably diminished in prevalence with all other craft-crimes, as McIntosh (1971) argues, since it is no longer necessary or advantageous for criminals to arm themselves with skill and technique, spiritually or practically, before taking what they want.

It is interesting to turn to the standard police manuals of criminal investigation to see what their comments on professionals are. Jackson (1962) discusses the methods used by professional shop thieves. In this disquisition attention is drawn to the way in which female professional shoplifters may have special pockets designed for the reception of stolen goods concealed beneath the dress. Jackson states (1962, p. 356):

> The essential thing in such cases is to search immediately the house of the suspected person as well as the houses of persons who have recently visited there. This often brings to light a regular depot for stolen property, a result of great value. Many other thefts are committed by unprofessional thieves ... who pick up anything they particularly fancy and place it in a bag, relying upon their appearance and impudence to bluff any assistant who challenges them.

In an interesting, although rather dated, section on thieves' accomplices, Jackson reviews the way in which professional thieves may steal from jewellers' shops. But in the fifth edition (1962) there is no detailed discussion of the most frequently encountered forms of modern shoplifting, indicating how recently the style of shop theft has changed. The forms Jackson discusses are all characterised by their subtlety and tortuous ingenuity, whereas modern professional theft is staggeringly bold in conception and is usually straightforward taking without subterfuge. Such theft as is now committed by professionals would have been impossible to perpetrate in the shops as they existed up to the 1950s. It has become possible today mainly as a result of a reduced staff to shop-floor square metre ratio, as well as to changes in shop geography and display technique and sales policy.

The bold, simple, criminal design or intention of the modern professional shoplifter has an advantage over earlier techniques. If the shoplifter is caught in the act of taking goods from a 'help-yourself' shop, he can always argue that he fully intended to pay for them, and was just about to if he had not been rudely and peremptorily interrupted by an over-zealous shop assistant. With earlier systems, if shoplifters were caught half-way through their crime, their *modus operandi* would give them away as thieves, in that no person without criminal intent would do the sort of things which they were trying to do. Also, social circumstances have changed to preclude many of the erstwhile methods of the professional. Perhaps today any jeweller would be suspicious of a man who asked for a purchase to be sent to an hotel of his own nomination and produced a visiting card as an indication of his identity! Nowadays, too, a woman acting in a suspicious way would instantly be stopped and searched, and if she were to dare to have special devices concealed underneath her clothing for the collection of goods they would be at once apparent on a search. (In fact, given changes in dress styles, and preferences for single rather than multi-layered clothing, it would be difficult for such receptacles to remain concealed anyway.) In the past shops would be reluctant to challenge and strip female shoppers. Now shops may have special search rooms and freely available female staff to do just this, without fearing that the reputation of their shop is likely to be damaged by subsequent adverse publicity arising from the incident.

As with any other form of organised crime, the modern professional relies on the fact that the aggressor always has the advantage. A determined 'attack', pressed home rapidly, skilfully and ruthlessly, can be simple in design in the modern shop, since such shops may have several doorways out, poorly lit areas, or 'protected' areas, such as mock-up kitchens or bathrooms, which provide needed cover where the shoplifter can tear off wrappings and labels and can repack the stolen goods in the favoured way. In the past shopping was an elaborate ritual where every move was expected and foreseeable. First the customer would enter, then make his request of the shopkeeper, who would then serve him. At every stage the shopkeeper functioned as a barrier to the shopper, first by literally standing in front of his goods arranged in racks behind him, with the counter between him and the shopper, so that nobody could reach the goods without requesting the shopkeeper's assistance, and second through making up parcels or wrapping goods in brown paper, finally placing them in the shopper's basket. Other than getting access to the goods through the shopkeeper, the shopper would only have been able to reach them through going behind the usually very substantial counter in front of the shopkeeper, which was seen as an unexpected and clear indication of criminal intent.

The goods themselves that were guarded by the shopkeeper were usually in a loose form, so that someone who wanted to buy nails or tea or tapers would first specify the quantity they required, and the shopkeeper would then draw this quantity from a larger stock; he would next make it up into a parcel, since usually, except in greengrocers' shops, people would not want small, loose items rattling around in their shopping bags. The process of selecting the appropriate amount or quantity and wrapping it would take time. Up until the 1950s in England people did not expect shopping to be a fast process, and they were quite prepared to wait for the customer in front of them to be served and for this to be time-consuming. The principal compensation was the opportunity for conversation and gossip while the process went on. Customers who wanted to rush in and rush out were rare, as were people who were only buying one item at a time. Now the situation has reversed, and there is an expectation that shopping can be fast and silent, rapid and rapacious, rather than slow and conversational. There are area exceptions to this, and shop-type exceptions to it, but the supermarket epitomises the quick, quiet type of shopping that has become so popular, where the shopper wanders around the shop in an autistic reverie, maintaining a religious silence and engaging in self-help, preoccupied as he is with supplying his own wants through the modern equivalent of foraging. In the past shoppers expected to be helped and advised as to the most suitable commodity, rather than having to find everything for themselves, and make guesses as to the appropriateness of the substances which they buy.

Now the barrier between the customer and the goods has disappeared, the result being that many customers waste time in trying to find things which may not be there, and, if they do manage to locate them, may buy a slightly inappropriate item merely for lack of advice. Had they been served or helped, then they might well have bought a more expensive item. The modern 'grubbing and foraging' type of shopping, where shoppers hunt desperately and despairingly for an article, fumbling and rummaging impatiently through piles of similar articles, watched with lethargic indifference by statuesque shop assistants immersed in their own dream-world, is of relatively recent origin.

When the shoplifter enters this arena of private foraging, he is indistinguishable from any ordinary shopper, and the arena itself appears almost to be organised in his favour, since foraging without paying is at a factual level only slightly different from foraging and paying. In the counter-service shop it is so much easier to see how necessary it is to pay the man who has helped choose the goods, gathered them in, and neatly parcelled them.

Community response to shoplifting

Generally the community response to all crime is interruptible indifference and ignorance. Ignorance is present for obvious reasons, the public have little idea of how much crime there is and how unflagging the activities of criminals are, and indifference arises because the identification and control of crime is seen to be the work of the trained specialists, the police. Both the indifference and the ignorance are interruptible in two main ways. First, when an individual (or his friends or relatives) experiences crime at first hand as a victim, then, understandably, he begins to care very much about the solution of the problem, and feels himself in the centre of the limelight and to be instantly possessed of expert knowledge because of his temporary awareness of a crime. Second, the veil of indifference and ignorance is lifted when there is a slow-dawning public awareness of a novel, notable, criminal figure operating, or perhaps a rash of crimes of a similar type occurring in a particular area. The media are responsible for the awareness, since it is they who warn the public of particular criminal activities in vivid, immediate ways which catch the imagination.

With both of these situations, 'crime at first hand', and what might be termed 'awakened outrage', the predominant reaction is emotion, varying with the form of the crime. The emotion seeks an outlet, and while the police are hurriedly trying to curb the crime or catch particular criminals there is a danger that scapegoats will be selected if people are not too frightened to do so. Inevitably the public have many 'wrong impressions' of criminals, just as they have wrong impressions of the police, or any other specialist occupational group; but the more dramatic the crime is presented as being, the less likely they are to either accept that their impressions are incorrect, or to change them. Eventually the temporary emotional outcry diminishes in force, and the matter is forgotten by all except the police who are still working on it, as it is displaced by new sources of concern which clamour for immediate attention. Public response to crime is emotional and it is mercurial, consisting of episodic, impotent outbursts at something which disturbs and worries people a good deal because they have suddenly discovered it in the newspapers or on the television.

These points apply even, and most especially, with serious violent crime. With lesser crime the amount of public inertia to be overcome is even greater and the ignorance and indifference less disruptible. For all crime, great or small, most people seem to feel that it is the job of the police to tackle it, usually alone. Accordingly the police are supposed to witness the crime, detect it, apprehend the criminals and spend time in law courts justifying publicly their behaviour and decisions. Members of the public are quite often put out, if not extremely indignant, on being asked to co-operate with the police by, for example, appearing in an identification parade, or having elimination fingerprints taken after a theft in their own home. They very often feel that the police should get on with it, whatever it is, by themselves and not intrude. Taking this line is of course a tacit mark of respect for, and trust in, the police, in that many people feel that they can do this work largely unaided. It is also an indication that people do not feel more than momentarily involved in the types of crime that occur, and do not see crime, or crime control, as having anything to do with them or their world at all for the most part. Until it is a 'crime at first hand', or an 'awakened outrage', situation, crime is fatalistically accepted as happening in the same way that ear, nose and throat disorders do.

Not surprisingly, then, but interestingly, the public as a whole appear to evince little interest in shoplifting. As a form of crime, it appears to be one which does not generate any great community anxiety. As each fresh shoplifting offence occurs, it does not promote a public outcry, and a demand for retributive punishment or vengeance, in fact it does not appear to generate any emotion whatsoever, except on the part of those immediately concerned with it, the victims, and not always then. Quite possibly this gives a very strong clue to the level of shoplifting in our society.

If the response of the community to it is not very positive and organised, then this must allow the crime to flourish and develop without hindrance. Single-victim crimes, where one person is injured or loses property as a result of criminal action, always attract more opprobrium than plural-victim crimes, where an organisation rather than the individuals who compose it is harmed, as when a company is defrauded or a bank or insurance house loses money through a crime committed against it. All the evidence is that professional and habitual criminals are very well aware of this, and tend to exploit if possible the relative lack of interest on the part of the public in plural-victim crimes. Parker and Allerton (1962, p. 92) describe a professional criminal's perception of public response. In a similar type of document, Crookston (1967, p. 139) goes further and states his disapproval of single-victim crimes on both a moral and an expedient basis.

A wave of (single-victim) burglaries in an area of a community results in hyper-organised collective response on the part of the police and the public until the criminals are caught or cease operations. However, patrols of vigilantes are not formed to deal with shoplifters. Apparently shoplifting is always associated in the mind of the public with plural victims, since reported instances of it do not, judging by reports in newspapers, attract high-emotional reactive responses, as do, for example, single-victim physical assaults, which produce the clearest unilateral public condemnation and result in rapid detection. Except for small numbers of individuals, little stigma attaches to being caught shoplifting, and again, according to public response as captured in and reflected by the mass media, shoplifting is accepted with fatalistic indifference rather than activist revulsion. For a community which produces a wide range of goods, and has thousands of retail outlets for them, theft of some of these goods is merely seen as an uninteresting daily event, rather than an activity which directly threatens the livelihood of individuals (which, if it occurs in small shops, it is likely so to do). However, although it may be a single-victim offence, it is invariably categorised as plural-victim, largely because it appears to occur more frequently in larger shops, and also because its impact is more concealed than is the case with a direct theft such as a street robbery.

The community as a whole has a stereotype of the shoplifter which it is interesting to examine. The stereotype functions due to ignorance. Those people who are in a position to know the amount of variation found in real-life shoplifting and shoplifters do not use it, but for those who know nothing of shoplifters, taking over the offered stereotype of the shoplifter which today's culture pushes towards them gives them an illusion of being worldly wise enough to interpret a phenomenon of which they are totally ignorant; it also helps them individually to generate subsequent opinions and attitudes about shoplifters.

In the stereotype, shoplifters are seen as middle-aged women, usually slightly mentally ill, and paradoxically, just because it *is* a stereotype, also possessed of great rationality, deviousness, cunning and technical ingenuity. It is assumed that the gains such (imaginary) people make are large, and that their depredations know no bounds, but that the numbers overall of such mythical shoplifters are small.

Stereotypic shoplifters are seen as rather comic and amusing because of their supposed dedication, audaciousness and seriousness of intent. They have frequently figured in novels and films, such as Elstree Studios' *Trouble in Store*, where the actress Dame Margaret Rutherford gave a masterly display of such a thief in operation in a large London shop, using a wide variety of devices concealed about her person to enable her to steal with impunity; for example, allowing her flowing sleeve to temporarily rest on the track of a miniature railway in the toy department, so that an electric train in motion ran into the sleeve and up her arm, whereupon she withdrew the sleeve still containing the toy train.

To the public, shoplifters are a harmless, eccentric, but not very numerous nuisance who tend to be concentrated in large London department stores, where they have a high velocity of circulation, and are soon caught because their daring surpasses their vigilance, and they are no match for sharp-eyed detectives.

The origin of this stereotype is a dated amalgam of pre-war police perceptions and snippets from the mass media derived from these. Emotionally disturbed middle-aged women, if they shoplift at all (which some will do, obviously), are of course, because the degree of emotional disturbance reduces their rationality, more likely to be caught quickly and more frequently than are other types of shoplifters. When caught, too, their relatives are more likely to make excuses for them, and this may even extend to legal sympathy being shown for them, all of which probably means more publicisation of the case. If this is so, as a community we tend to hear proportionately more in the newspapers about the middle-aged, emotionally distressed, female shoplifter than we do about other, less controversial cases, where less people are prepared to spring to the aid of the thief, or bend over backwards to be fair to him. If the public hear more about such shoplifters they naturally tend to assume that these cases constitute the majority of shoplifting charges, all of which would function to reinforce the stereotype.

Given the pressure to accept an incorrect interpretation of who shoplifts, and given the content of that incorrect interpretation, it is not surprising that the community at large is substantially indifferent to the presence of shoplifters in its midst. If the real population did conform to the stereotype it would certainly not constitute any great threat to established commerce.

The presence of this stereotype has a 'masking' effect, since the general public find difficulties in believing that it is untrue, once it has persisted for long enough. Middle-aged women shoplifters also become a rubber scapegoat, a scapegoat for others' crimes, but relatively uninjured by public opprobrium, because they are supposed to be sad women.

The overall outcome is that there is a very low level of anxiety in the community about the crime of shoplifting: people are simply not aware of the quantity that obtains, nor are they aware of how widespread it is as a crime-form, largely due to the masking effect of the stereotype. This of course allows and facilitates the activities of shoplifters, since they do not face a high degree of organised public hostility towards their actions. In turn the low level of stigmatisation that attaches to being called a shoplifter in the courts can also be seen to function not to inhibit would-be 'prodromal' shoplifters from practising and dabbling in the crime.

This means that there is very little functioning to prevent people from shoplifting, or to immunise them against ever committing it, apart from domestic morality acquired in the home, and reinforced inside a moral vacuum. Where this domestic morality is not present then people will shoplift if they can get away with it, since in utilitarian terms the penalties are slight.

This situation has been reinforced by economic plenty, where the economic sector has produced millions of pounds worth of consumer goods, and where the retail outlets for these are widely scattered, so a very large amount of shoplifting can occur before it is noticed. There is a time-lag before shoplifting as an economic effect begins to 'bite', and by the time it finally has been noticed and is no longer concealed inside a shrinkage figure it is then too late, since shoplifting can have become customary behaviour for many, and the means of justifying it and rationalising it will have been developed.

This is the state that we have now arrived at, when crime prevention in relation to shoplifting encounters, amongst other things, resistance developed through some years of concealed practice when shoplifting has been culturally invisible.

Community disposal of shoplifters

The most logical way for a community to treat the problem posed by shoplifting offenders would be, in the case of each individual offender, to first ensure that he is capable of distinguishing right from wrong. If he is, then tell him that shoplifting is wrong and criminal in such a way that he can see the reason for this, agree with it, and be convinced of it, and carry out such a process in an environment where temptation exists. Thus he can become accustomed to living and working in society without stealing from shops, and without constantly feeling that he can and should slip under the wire and steal, providing that nobody catches him at it.

In practice what happens is far removed from this kind of rationale. Most shoplifters when caught are fined, some are put on probation, and a tiny number are still sent to prison. It is possible to argue that the introduction of treatment by fining is rather shortsighted as a treatment technique for shoplifters, and as prophylactically unsound as the use of imprisonment. In the case of the small number of shoplifters who are sent to prison, the advantage for the community is that while they are there they are withdrawn from the world of temptation, but on the other hand, in prison they are not usually given any instruction, least of all moral instruction, indicating that shoplifting is wrong and should not be engaged in. What might then be expected to happen is that at the end of a sentence spent incarcerated in, in all probability, an overcrowded local prison, the shoplifter is released and continues to shoplift.

The drawback to the use of fines as a means of treating shoplifters is that their use is likely to make possible and encourage for shoplifters a form of utilitarianism which does not operate to society's advantage. The rational shoplifter can weigh the hypothetical fine payable if he gets caught with what he can take illegally from shops before he arrives at his ultimate position in court (and as a bonus, he can further assume statistically that his appearance there anyway is not a certainty), and on this rational, utilitarian basis continue to shoplift. What is dubious about the use of fines for shoplifters is that fining reduces the reaction to the crime to a monetary issue, and does not efficiently include reference to morals or the wrongness of the act. Being caught and punished in a law court by a fine can easily slip into a morality-free materialist transaction for the shoplifter. The shoplifter who is punished by a fine is never going to learn that it is wrong to shoplift, instead he is going to learn that it is right to calculate.

Long-term management of the problem on this basis would include rejecting the use of fines or imprisonment in the broad run of cases, arguing that such approaches only represent temporary interruptions in shoplifting careers, and concentrating instead on other types of treatment which should include (at least) straightforward moral instruction in an environment where temptation to steal is present, to make it a proper 'live' test.

If it could be shown that there are any factors in modern retail sales practices which actively encourage shoplifting, a further possibility from the point of view of curtailing shoplifting, approaching the problem from an entirely different direction, might be to consider the wisdom of legislating against the use of such practices. This of course would be a drastic measure, and would have attached to it numerous ethical and economic question marks, and it goes without saying that before even considering such action careful proof of the causal role of the practices in question would need to be adduced.

For various reasons, especially those outlined in the introduction to this study, the research hypotheses are focused not on specific offender motivation issues at all but on victim issues. There is of course an enormous possible range of hypotheses in relation to shoplifting. For example, those relating shoplifting to wider cultural attitudes, as well as to the economy, aside from those dealing with qualities possessed by the offender.

I decided to restrict myself to a group of interlinked topics which when tested should offer a way of seeing shoplifting largely in terms of availability and opportunity, as well as providing a possible victim-prevention bonus. As was mentioned above, if the victim can be removed from the potential arena that includes the crime and the criminal, then no crime occurs. (This is ignoring the possibility that the would-be criminal will then find another victim in a different arena of operations, of course.) Through testing some specific hypotheses, it is hoped perhaps to learn more about possible ways of achieving this victim-removal, or victim-prevention, goal. Below are listed the hypotheses that I wished to test, together with some notes on their formulation and the reasons for their inclusion.

1. *Shops with counter service will have less shoplifting than self-service shops.*
This is arguing that counter-service shops exercise greater control over the activities of the shopper, who in turn is prepared to accept this, because of the greater rewards offered in such shops, such as advice, interest and conversation.

2. *The larger the shop, the more the shoplifting.*
This argues that small shops can contain the problem more easily, partly because of the scale of their operations, partly because of the self-interest of the person who is running the shop, and partly because of reduced impersonality and low social distance. It is also extremely unlikely that customers who hold that shoplifting is ideologically justified, or morally justified, would feel this to be the case where small shops such as one-man businesses are concerned.

3. *Shops occupying sites in city centres are more likely to suffer from shoplifters than shops in outlying areas.*
Centrally placed shops are in areas where there is anyway a high velocity of circulation of shoppers, and concomitantly they are more at risk to shoplifting. In addition it is more likely that people who wish to steal will do so from central shops rather than from outlying ones, because of the more lavish displays of goods in central shops, and because of improved high-speed escape routes, and hiding places subsequent to the event, for example. This is hypothesising that city-centre shops act as a magnet for all shoppers, including shoplifters.

4. *Shops selling luxuries are more likely to suffer more from shoplifters than those selling necessities.*
Aristotle put forward the idea that it is excess, not poverty, which produces crime. The assumption here is that luxuries tempt the thief more than necessities. This would suggest that fancy goods shops, shops selling motor-car accessories, and food, clothing and adornment luxuries will be more at risk than those selling more mundane goods such as meat, fish and bread.

5. *Shops that have high rates of shoplifting will tend to blame outside agencies for this.*
The outside agencies are the public in general (supposedly lacking

in morality) and the police in general (supposedly less than efficient). The hypothesis is arguing that high-risk shops will have owners who tend to blame outside agencies in the way described, rather than accepting that such high rates as they experience may be chiefly due to the type of good which they sell, or may be exacerbated, or even substantially produced, by the sheer extent of the temptation, if not better termed provocation, resulting from the pursuit of impulse sales policies. The craze for the 'help-yourself' shop, as it was originally called, undoubtedly increases the *risk* of theft, but more directly and immediately it has attractions for businessmen, who are not pre-eminently concerned with morality but with risk-taking, entrepreneurial activity of a directly competitive sort. If the businessman's aim is to poach customers from a rival shop in as efficient a way as possible, then in a situation where few shops are using impulse purchase policies, those that do will filch customers from competitors more adroitly, and in the short run show higher rates of profit as a result, to recompense them for their risk taking.

Shoplifting in such a shop presents a reminder of the logical conclusion to all of this, as well as the blatancy of it, and I am hypothesising that the form of the moral resolution of the problem from the shopkeeper's point of view is to blame outside society, and specific groups within it, rather than himself. Perhaps it is easier for a shop-owner to say, 'the public are immoral', rather than to accept that his own sales practices can be extremely provocative. It is easier to do this than ask why certain shops next door to his own do *not* have such high rates of theft. If all the public really were immoral, then no shop would be exempt from the attentions of thieves. The police cannot, as well as all their other tasks, be expected to police not only the streets and the pavements, but also the interiors of the shops on them. Indeed, no shop-owner would want the police to make a practice of checking his shop for thieves, unless called in for a specific purpose. Such a practice would be seen as a threat to liberty and freedom. Yet some shop-owners perhaps can still argue that the police are not efficient when dealing with shoplifters.

6. *The more heterogeneous the clientele in any one shop, the more shoplifting is likely to occur.*

This is arguing that shops with a homogeneous clientele are less likely to experience difficulties than shops where many different types of customer are likely to be present. I am assuming here that norms of shopping behaviour and customer appearance are more easily defined in homogeneous shops, which operate to the disadvantage of the casual shoplifter. In shops with a wide range of different types of customer it is much harder for shopkeepers and shop assistants to know what 'normal' shopping behaviour consists of. In some instances, then, if this were true, it would argue for an immunity against shoplifting possessed by the specialist shop, and it would certainly place the department store and the supermarket in a high-risk group.

3

Shoplifting in Exeter

The economic gravity of the problem of shoplifting needs no emphasis. Carter (1974) estimates the social cost of theft overall in England and Wales to be about £650 million, and the contribution of shop theft to this figure roughly £400 million. These can only be rough guides to the widespread nature of the offence. Much work has already been done on shoplifting both in this country and America, for example Gibbens (1962), Cameron (1964), Belson (1969) and the more recent Home Office study (1973).

In this study which was carried out in Exeter, I have been concerned to investigate especially the extent to which shoplifting is largely victim-precipitated, and what the attitude and reaction of the victim is to this crime. First, data collected on the extent and concentration of the offence is presented, then data on offender characteristics, and lastly the information on victim reaction, and the extent to which victim-precipitation is a trigger for shoplifting offences.[1]

Exeter is a small cathedral city of approximately 100,000 people, with a rural hinterland. In the commercial sense it has been until very recently old-fashioned in its marketing techniques, supermarkets being a relatively recent introduction, most having arrived in the last seven years. For this reason it was presumed that shoplifting as an offence form would not be highly developed and systematised, and that the reaction of the commercial sector to it would be flexible.

This is primarily an interview study, but much information has been most helpfully provided by the police forces in the area about the crime, both in the form of statistical information and discussions with senior police officials. I make no special claim for the worth of the study; it is simply an attempt to collect facts about extent of offence, offenders and victims, and working with these to try and map the crime-form, reconstructing the 'blanks', where these exist, from the developing factual framework.

In general of course with shoplifting, we have a very much to be expected offence, given the economic system and the pressures to consume in a highly industrialised community with a competitive individualised ethos. No shoplifting can exist in a community without trade or shops. Given full shops and strong pressures from the culture and the media to acquire consumer goods, then it becomes naïve to suppose that shoplifting exists to supply simple necessities. It seems much more probable that it exists to supply luxuries, and to gratify various psychological needs which cannot otherwise be met in the relatively stable, secure, routinely patterned existence which most shoplifters customarily are involved in when not shoplifting. Testing propositions such as these becomes more formidable the more shoplifters there are.

In a sense, shoplifting proper has only recently 'begun' in the area I was investigating, and for both shoplifters and shopkeepers alike it is a novel experience, with both sides making many false starts and many mistakes. As yet there is little that is sophisticated about shoplifting in Exeter. Its tentative emergence has made the investigation all the more stimulating, since both 'keepers' and 'lifters' alike are unfamiliar with the moves to be made. Before dealing with the findings under the specific headings outlined above, the methods used will first be briefly discussed.

Information on shoplifting in Exeter was collected in three ways as follows:

1. *Shopkeeper sample*

A 10 per cent sample of shopkeepers was drawn and each shopkeeper was interviewed. A five-year-old trade directory was used as a sampling frame, which consisted of a list of shops stratified by type. Categories of shops (such as wholesalers) which could not be subject to shoplifting were excluded, although it is interesting to reflect on the origin of the immunity of such shops. A 10 per cent sample was then drawn from this frame, consisting of 80 shops in the city centre, suburbs and outlying villages. The main bias, which was desirable and intentional, was in favour of shopkeepers who had survived for five years, and who should, because of this, have stabilised experience of shoplifting on their premises. Letters were then written to the shops drawn in the sample explaining the purpose of the work, and requesting an interview. Out of the 80, interviews were held with 61, there being one refusal and 18 uncontactables. Up to six call-backs were used, and some substitution was necessary. The interview was structured and lasted approximately twenty minutes. The shops were divided into three types, those totally self-service, those counter-service only, and those with mixed service (part counter-service and part self-service). Shops in the sample were distributed as shown in Tables 4 and 5.

Table 4 *Exeter shoplifting: Distribution of shops in the sample*

Type of service	City centre	Outskirts	Total
Counter service	16	12	28
Self-service	10	6	16
Mixed service	6	11	17
Total	32	29	61

Table 5 *Exeter shoplifting: Size of shops in the sample*

Size (number of assistants)	Counter service	Self-service	Mixed service	Total
Small (one assistant)	3	–	1	4
Medium (two to four assistants)	19	8	12	39
Large (more than four assistants)	6	8	4	18
Total	28	16	17	61

2. Offender sample

A 10 per cent sample of offenders was drawn, and data on these was obtained from police files. The method of choosing the sample of offenders' files from police records was as follows. The total population of shoplifting *cases* (each case involving possibly more than one offender) known to the police in the Exeter area in 1975 was stratified by age into eight groups. Within each stratum a 10 per cent sample was chosen proportionate to the observed age distribution in the population. This was done by putting the numbers into a hat. The resulting distribution is shown below in Table 6.

Table 6 *Exeter shoplifting: Proportions in the offender sample*

Age group	Frequency in total population	Number chosen for sample
Up to 9	11	1
10–15	168	16
16–20	101	8
21–30	92	7
31–40	75	6
41–50	67	5
51–60	45	3
61 and over	56	4
Total	615	50

NOTE: The frequency total for the entire population is greater than the total of cases (519), because it includes *all those* jointly charged. The sample proportions are calculated on this total. The age profile was derived from all offenders. Fifty cases were abstracted where the principal offender's age distribution is proportional to that observed in the age profile for the general population. (For each case more than one offender may be involved.)

3. *Offence records*

Records of shoplifting offences known to the police in 1975 were used. Information was drawn from them using police computer facilities. The major problem of course with using these statistics is one of under-reporting, which in turn means lack of representativeness. Very little of the shoplifting that obtains comes to the attention of the police, and that which does is of necessity rather 'special' shoplifting. Shopkeepers are often unwilling to take a case to the police because they feel it is a disgrace to have the firm's name in the local newspaper (and future customers might be deterred by this), or because they feel that there is very little the police can do, or little that the courts *will* do, or because they fear a full-scale investigation (especially the effect it may have on their staff). In addition, for some companies it is policy not to involve the police at all.

Both shopkeepers and police agree that known cases of shoplifting only represent a fraction of all that does occur, and that what is known to the shopkeeper is not necessarily told to the police. Of necessity with shoplifting, the police tend only to be aware of crimes committed either by professionals, or bizarre and unusual offences, or offences committed by the unintelligent and the slow-moving!

When these three types of offences are put together they may pass muster as a column of figures, but they do not indicate the real problem, which is not professional, bizarre or slow-moving, since shopkeepers *themselves* are often not aware of the real problem in their shops, and if they are, most do not like to trouble or involve the police.[2] Only the most blatant (persistent), unskilful, unintelligent or unusual cases go forward for prosecution.

The main findings and supporting evidence are now presented, and inevitably, for the sake of brevity, a mass of interesting material has had to be omitted from this section.

Extent and concentration of shoplifting offences

Area distribution and volume

Of the shoplifting offences known to the police which occurred in 1975 in Exeter and its suburbs, the greatest concentration was in the central shopping area (High Street zone), not surprisingly, where 80·48 per cent of known offences occurred. Table 7 below summarises distribution. This is of course only a fraction of all shoplifting that occurred during this year. As evidence for this we could take the information provided by shopkeepers from the sample when asked to estimate the number of instances of shoplifting that they experienced throughout the last year. This sample *alone* reported an absolute minimum of 417 cases in the last year. Of all shops, only 18 per cent had no case of shoplifting at all in the last year, 68 per

Table 7 *Exeter shoplifting: Area distribution of known shoplifting offences (offences known to the police, 1975)*

Area	Frequency of offences	%
Whipton and Pinhoe	9	1·79
Wonford, Countess Wear and Topsham	2	0·40
Pennsylvania	1	0·20
Exwick, Alphington	25	4·98
St David's zone	46	9·16
Heavitree zone	15	2·99
High Street zone	404	80·48
Total	502	100·00

cent of the self-service shops had 20 or more cases a year, compared with 35 per cent of the mixed-service shops, and none of the counter-service shops. None of the self-service shops escaped a case last year, whereas 32 per cent of the counter-service shops had no case.

Another index of the inevitable under-reporting that must occur with an offence such as this is the 'recency of last offence' information that was collected from the shopkeeper sample, and is presented below in Table 8.

Table 8 *Exeter shoplifting: Date of last offence of shoplifting (shopkeeper sample)*

Type of shop	Date of last offence					
	Within last week	8–28 days	More than one month	No case	Don't know	Total
Self-service	9	2	5	–	–	16
Counter service	1	–	9	9	9	28
Mixed service	5	–	10	1	1	17
Total	15	2	24	10	10	61

Occurrence of last-known offence

Twenty-four per cent of all shops had a case within the last week, but taking the self-service shops alone, 56 per cent had a case within the last week. Twenty-nine per cent of the mixed-service shops had at least one case within the last week, whereas only 3 per cent of the counter-service shops had. In fact 32 per cent of the counter-service shops had no case at all, as against 5·8 per cent for the mixed-service shops. All self-service shops had a case. All the indications are that there is much more shoplifting than comes to the attention of the police, and this is discussed more fully in the section on victim reaction. Suffice it to say here that detection rates (that is, instances where the offender was apprehended) for those offences which are reported are extremly good, which is perhaps not surprising in view of the nature of the offence. The percentage of the 1975 reported cases that were detected was 88·44. The official figure is 4,002 for all thefts from shops and stalls known to the police to have been committed in the two counties, the number detected being 3,442.[3] The detection rate here of 85·58 per cent is very similar to that for the Exeter area just quoted.

Premises where offence occurred

As far as concentration by shop type is concerned, the distribution is shown in Table 9. Although this information shows a strong concentration in both department stores and small, one-man shops, it must not be forgotten that it cannot be regarded in isolation from preparedness to prosecute.

Table 9   *Exeter shoplifting: Premises where offence occurred (offences known to the police, 1975)*

Type of shop	Frequency of known offences	%
Sub-post office	1	0·2
Café	1	0·2
Mobile display unit	1	0·2
Market stall	2	0·4
Jeweller	4	0·8
Outfitter	22	4·37
Ordinary shop	45	8·94
Chemist	67	13·32
Small shop	134	26·64
Large department store (including supermarkets)	226	44·93
Total	503	100·00

Detection of shoplifting

Table 10 below presents data on rates of detection. Detection in shoplifting is mainly done by shop staff, not by the police, because it is initially an internal matter. This might lead one to assume that large stores with longer periods between stock-taking and less self-interested assistants would have higher rates of undetected crime. In fact this was not the case, it is actually smaller shops which have higher rates of undetected crime, perhaps due to their being more unprepared, and not really seeing shoplifting as a problem.

Table 10 *Exeter shoplifting: Rate of detection by shop type (offences known to the police, 1975)*

Type of shop	Frequency of undetected cases
Sub-post office	–
Café	–
Mobile display unit	–
Market stall	1 out of 2
Jeweller	1 out of 4
Outfitter	8 out of 22
Ordinary shop	1 out of 45
Chemist	3 out of 67
Small shop	27 out of 134
Large department store (including supermarkets)	13 out of 226
Total	54

The timing of offences

Monthly incidence figures, presented in Table 11 below, show a crude monthly average of 41·75 offences. The clear 'highs' are in April (12·38 per cent) and in the pre-Christmas buildup in November (12·18 per cent). 'Lows' occur in January (5·18 per cent) and in August (4·99 per cent), when conceivably holidaying may disrupt routine shoplifting, although the flow of people to and from the area is clearly two-way! Data on monthly incidence from the shops gives a slightly different picture. Each shopkeeper was asked to say which were the times of the year when there is most shoplifting. The winter was indicated by 32·8 per cent and the summer by 15·63 per cent as peak times for shoplifting. The two obvious peaks, just before Christmas and during the summer, are of course both busy times and sales times. But 40·63 per cent of shops either had no idea when peaks occurred, or else maintained that there was an even spread throughout the year. The information on daily distribution of offences is shown in Table 12.

Daily distribution of offences

A quarter of all offences known to the police occur on Saturday, when there are in any case more people on the streets than normal.

Table 11 *Exeter shoplifting: Monthly distribution of offences (offences known to the police, 1975)*

Month	Frequency	%
January	26	5·18
February	47	9·38
March	37	7·39
April	62	12·38
May	46	9·18
June	42	8·38
July	46	9·18
August	25	4·99
September	34	6·79
October	32	6·39
November	61	12·18
December	43	8·58
Total	501	100·00

Table 12 *Exeter shoplifting: Daily distribution of offences (offences known to the police, 1975)*

Day	Frequency	%
Monday	72	14·52
Tuesday	81	16·33
Wednesday	53	10·69
Thursday	63	12·70
Friday	97	19·56
Saturday	125	25·20
Sunday	5	1·00
Total	496	100·00

When shopkeepers were asked to indicate which days in the week were likely to attract most offences, data obtained was not particularly useful, beyond suggesting an even spread of offences throughout the week. This information did reveal that days early in the week are not seen as days of peak activity, it also hinted at the much-mentioned buildup towards the end of the week. At this time there are more people in the shops anyway, so that there can be an expectation of greater shoplifting, since the population at risk is so much larger.

Shoplifting: Controlling a Major Crime

To try and see what the peak times are during the day, each shopkeeper was asked to specify times when there was more likely to be shoplifting. The results showed that 36·9 per cent of shopkeepers considered that there was peak shoplifting activity during the period 12 noon to 2 p.m. During this 'lunch-time' period there is a relatively high density and velocity of circulation of shoppers, as off-duty shop assistants swell the crowd. Broadly, shoplifters are stated to prefer busy shops, so that 'lunch-time' becomes a very high risk time.

Time of day when offence occurred

In the offender sample, the time of day when offences were committed is shown in Table 13 below. There was no particular age-group preference for time of day. Taking the morning up to 1 p.m., 30·4 per cent of cases in the sample were committed during this time. From 1 p.m. onwards, 69 per cent of the sample cases occurred, with the greatest concentration between 2 and 4 p.m., when 45·7 per cent of offences were committed. The expected concentration at lunch-time does not appear, but it must be remembered that although much shoplifting may be expected at this time, there are less staff present to report it, and due to the press of people in particular shops it may be much harder to observe.

Table 13 *Exeter shoplifting: Time of day when offence occurred (offender sample)*

Time	Frequency of offences	%
9–10 a.m.	2	4·3
10–11	5	10·9
11–12 noon	3	6·5
12–1 p.m.	4	8·7
1–2	5	10·9
2–3	11	24·0
3–4	10	21·7
4–5	6	13·0
Total	46	100.0

NOTE: In four cases the time was unknown

This kind of information on monthly, daily and hourly rates of shoplifting must not blind one to the realisation that shoplifting goes on all day and all year round, and observed 'peaks' in it relate largely to styles of reporting.

Offender characteristics

Sex of shoplifters

Shopkeepers were asked to estimate who in their opinion in their shop was responsible for most shoplifting, men alone, women alone, children alone, or combinations of these. From this information the greatest shoplifters seem to be children, where 24·5 per cent of shops reported them as the majority-type shoplifter.[4] Sixteen per cent of shops indicated that their greatest problem came from both sexes equally, and only 8 per cent of shops reported women as being the most active shoplifters. Rather significantly, 34 per cent of shops had no clear view on the sex of the shoplifter. The breakup for the sexes from the offender sample is shown in Table 14. It will be

Table 14 *Exeter shoplifting: Sex and age of offenders (offender sample)*

Age	Male	Female	Total
Up to 15	19	12	31
16–20	2	5	7
21–30	2	6	8
31–40	4	3	7
41–50	1	2	3
51–60	5	1	6
61 and over	1	2	3
Total	34	31	65

recalled that the proportions in the age-grades in this sample were determined in relation to total population proportions. Bearing in mind that there are more women in shops than men, and that women ought to be easier to apprehend than men, it is surprising that there are so many men in this sample.

Age of shoplifters

Ages of known offenders convicted of shoplifting in Exeter in 1975 were as shown below in Table 15. Frequencies here refer to instances of conviction, not individuals. One person can be convicted a number of times, so that there is a 'revolving door' to use Pittman and Gordon's phrase (1958), but if anything, the revolving door problem helps us to see more clearly in absolute terms the contribution to shoplifting made by each age-grade. The only way in which it is a handicap is if we were concerned to know the actual number of individuals involved. The real number of individuals will obviously be less than this list, made up from all a person's convictions, indicates. The concentration in the age-grade 'up to 15' is reflected also in the information provided on age by shopkeepers when asked to indicate the age of shoplifters. Here the probability is that shopkeepers selectively do not notice some age groups of shoplifters (see the section on recognition of a shoplifter). Estimates show a heavy concentration in the age-grade 'up to 15' (27·87 per cent), which ties in with ages derived from offence records. Twenty-four per cent of shopkeepers wisely regard shoplifters as being 'of all ages'. The fact that youngsters are probably easier to observe and catch is also germane here.

Table 15   Exeter shoplifters: Ages of shoplifters
(offences known to the police, 1975)

Age group	Frequency	%
Up to 15	179	29·10
16–20	101	16·42
21–30	92	14·96
31–40	75	12·20
41–50	67	10·89
51–60	45	7.32
61 and over	56	9·11
Total	615	100·00

Occupation of offenders

Data on occupation of offenders obtained from the offender sample is contained in Table 16. Although this is only data from one sample of offenders, taken with the information already established on age, it seems clear that schoolchildren preponderate, and that the contribution made by them is steady and sizeable. Due to the small size of this sample it was not possible to try and reproduce Gibbens's findings (1962, p. 155), that 'shoplifting is committed with unusual frequency by social classes I and II.'

Table 16 Exeter shoplifting: Occupation of offenders (offender sample)

Occupation	Frequency	%
Schoolchildren	30	46
Students	4	6
Housewives	5	8
Unemployed	15	23
Other	11	17
Total	65	100

Whether the offences were committed alone or not

Table 17 shows the numbers preferred in the offender groups crossed by age. Frequencies given represent all offenders involved. Most individuals (55·41 per cent) committed their offences alone. Offences were committed by a pair in 34·47 per cent of cases. 'Pairing' was most popular among 10–15-year-olds, where 50·60 per cent of all offences committed were carried out in pairs. This accords fairly well with Debuyst's finding (1960), that children under the age of 13 prefer to steal in pairs, and those over this age steal alone. Only 9·76 per cent of all offenders committed their offence as one of a group of three, four or five people.

Method of shoplifting

With the offender sample, no particularly special methods of shoplifting were apparent, but it is not to be expected that 'high technology' shoplifting would show up as well as cruder and more unsuccessful varieties. Shopkeepers were asked how the shoplifting that they were aware of was usually carried out. While 24·59 per cent of shopkeepers said that shoplifters would buy articles at the same time as stealing others, 16·39 per cent of shopkeepers said that

Table 17 *Exeter shoplifting: Preference for isolation or ganging among shoplifting offenders (offences known to the police, 1975)*

Age	Number of offences committed alone	Number of offences committed in pairs	Number of offences committed in a group of three or more
Up to 9	1	1	1
10–15	45	40	10
16–20	54	8	3
21–30	65	4	–
31–40	36	14	–
41–50	49	4	–
51–60	40	1	–
61 and over	48	1	–
Groupings of mixed ages	–	33	6
Total number of offences committed	338	106	20

shoplifters would not buy as well, but would steal without paying and walk or run out of the shop. Most frequently, in the detected cases, other articles are purchased as well, and simply put into the shopping bag. As with the offender sample, those detected have a 'low' technology.

However, there are exceptions to this, and various special problems. Many self-service food shops are plagued by customers eating the food as they go around shopping (one shopkeeper informant said that he himself did this regularly, and would present his apple cores at the check-out counter!). Especially in small self-service food shops, staff complain of mothers allowing children to eat their fill of sweets while they are in the shop.

Shops selling different types of goods have different and special problems to contend with. In ironmongers, power tools are usually kept chained, but shoplifters will frequently cut through the chains. Where electric irons with a hook-type handle are kept 'secure' by having a chain passed through the loop of coiled flex, then shoplifters will cut through the electric flex and take the iron. In shoe shops, people will leave their old shoes behind in the display box, and wear the new shoes out of the shop, sometimes replacing their children's shoes in the same way without paying. In mens' clothes shops, frequently a man will wear new trousers which he has paid for out of the shop, and will conceal another pair of trousers (which he has not paid for) under his old trousers in his shopping bag. In one motor accessories shop an instance was reported of a male and female pair shoplifting together, where the woman hooked objects on to elasticated hooks concealed beneath her skirt, while the assistant's attention was being distracted by the man. In a food shop, the manager's attention was drawn to the repeated arm twitching of a handicapped middle-aged man wearing a leg-iron; when later he was searched, the man was found to be wearing a jacket with 12-inch (30·5 cm) pockets sewn under the arms, and his supposed nervous twitching had resulted in numbers of packets of biscuits and yoghourts being deposited in the pockets. As one manager said, 'I say to my staff, shoplifters could take the trousers off you and you would not notice.'

However, most shoplifting is just 'taking without paying', placing the object in a shopping bag along with other purchases. Instances of special method are rare. On a rather different point, instances of crankish shoplifting are sufficiently common as to have high nuisance value. For example, one shop reported that every day a man would come in to make purchases and as he left steal a packet of wrapped sweets which he could well afford to pay for. In a china shop it was reported that once a week a china horse would be stolen, and this practice continued until finally there were no more horses left in stock. In a food shop, milk left out for sale would be stolen in bulk by one man, but only the gold top, never the ordinary type. In a toy shop, where it was claimed that the most frequent method of shoplifting was for a man with a baby on his arm to use the baby as 'cover' for theft, a case was mentioned of a lad eager to steal an electric train from the shop window who rushed into the shop, and leapt through the (very high) window display, scattering stacks of boxes in all directions in order to steal the toy.

It was frequently mentioned that fashions in clothes, especially clothes for women, have a bearing on method. When it was fashionable for young women to wear cloaks and ponchos, such clothes provided greater concealment than does the wearing of thin, single-layer clothing. This is a further point in support of the argument that there is increased shoplifting in the autumn and winter, when most people wear heavier, multi-layered clothing.[5]

Goods selected for theft

The goods stolen by individuals in the offender sample are shown in Table 18. There is a wider scatter for male offences among the

Table 18 *Exeter shoplifting: Goods stolen (offender sample)*

Type of goods	Males	Females	Total	%
Stationery	6	–	6	9·23
Books	2	1	3	4·62
Clothing	5	7	12	18·46
Cosmetics	5	10	15	23·07
Food	11	10	21	32·31
Money	1	–	1	1·54
Other	4	3	7	10·77
Total	34	31	65	100·00

categories, with a greater concentration for women on food and cosmetics. Overall, the most popular category detected is food, followed by cosmetics and clothing. When the shopkeeper sample were asked to specify what exactly shoplifters took from their shops, in the reports made, there was a strong concentration on luxury goods. Few people took cheap necessities, most took expensive luxuries. But, as one manager said, 'they take everything, they would take the shop if they could!' In terms of types of goods and type of shop it becomes easy to construct a list of shops at risk. Table 19 represents the broad pattern of theft as presented by the shopkeeper sample.

Amount stolen

The figures from the shopkeeper sample show that 31 per cent of shops lost on average less than £1 worth of goods per incident, whereas only 11 per cent of shops had an average incident value of over £10; 54 per cent of shops were averaging a loss of £5 or under

Table 19 *Exeter shoplifting: Objects reported as most commonly stolen (shopkeeper sample)*

	Shop	Goods taken from shops
High-risk shops (where shoplifting occurs daily)	Department stores Food shops Confectioners Electrical and radio Ironmongers Motor accessories Ladies' clothing Booksellers	Most small items at risk Pre-packaged foodstuffs Cigars, chocolate bars Cassette radios Tools, especially power tools Gloves, sunglasses, instruments Tights Stationery
Medium-risk shops (where shoplifting occurs intermittently)	Chinaware Wines and spirits House furnishers Chemists Men's clothing	Ornaments Miniatures of spirits Display objects Sundries (not medicines) Ties, trousers
Low-risk shops (where there is virtually no shoplifting)	Butchers Fishmongers Greengrocers Jewellers Office equipment Shoe shops Tailors	Negligible Negligible Negligible Rings Negligible Footwear Small items

per incident. This ties in fairly well with the official figures, where an analysis of thefts from shops and stalls is given. See Table 20.

Professionalism among offenders

There was little evidence of professionalism among shoplifters, perhaps not surprisingly. Professionalism has to be distinguished from premeditated and calculating raids by those amateurs who have a clear objective. Professionals usually operate in gangs, hiring a house for the purpose, placing a car centrally, and loading it up on a daily 'pillage' basis. They are highly organised, but the extent of their organisation necessitates predictability, and it is this which

Table 20 Amount stolen in pounds sterling by detected shoplifters in Devon and Cornwall (1975)

	Under £5	£5–£25	£25–£100	£100–£500	£500–£1,000	£1,000 and over	Total
Number stealing from shops and stalls	2,699	860	335	98	2	8	4,002

NOTE: These are figures for the two counties together, not just for Exeter. They clearly show that the average theft in 1975 was under £5 in value.

SOURCE: The Chief Constable's Annual Report for Devon and Cornwall Constabulary (1975, p. 57)

means that they are soon caught, since it is very easy to set up security systems predicated upon their rationality. Additionally, apart from things like early warning networks, the Travelling Criminals' Index usually gives police in the South West ample advance warning of the approach of shoplifters through Eastern counties. Estimates of the numbers of professional shoplifters hover around the 2 per cent of all mark (Gibbens (1962) estimated 6·2 per cent).

Undeniably, many shopkeepers feel that they are being persecuted by professionals when in fact they are merely being raided by calculating amateurs. Shopkeepers are agreed that professionals take high-value goods only, and in large quantities, and rely heavily on having a group of accomplices who can distract the attention of shop assistants. The fact, noticed by many shopkeepers, that shoplifters will often try to shoplift at lunchtime (hoping that most of the staff are at lunch or too busy to observe them), or first thing on opening in the morning (hoping that most of the staff are sleepy), or last thing before closing (hoping that most of the staff are keen to go quickly and cash up) does not make these shoplifters professionals.

Professionalism of the type referred to in Cameron's work (1964) was not assessed as anything other than extremely rare in the Exeter area. A few instances were mentioned of the mail-order shoplifter, who shoplifts with a 'shopping list' to supply customers who buy from her, thinking that they are buying from a genuine mail-order firm rather than an isolated shoplifter, but police and shopkeepers argued for the rarity of such instances.

Today the shoplifter can be anyone, there are no features of dress, age or sex or economic status that help us to identify him, and trying to do so leads quickly to stereotyping (if not scapegoating). For example, the prejudice that many shopkeepers feel against gangs of youngsters of the age of fifteen or so certainly has a slight factual basis; however, concentrating on this group easily leads to underestimation of the shoplifting done by older age groups. Shoplifting can be done by almost anyone: in this sample, as well as a case of two eighty-year-olds shoplifting with a ten-year-old child, there was a case of a five-year-old.

Previous criminality of offenders

The distribution of previous offences for offenders with shoplifting convictions showed that just over 32 per cent of all offenders in the offender sample had previous convictions (not necessarily for shoplifting), 66 per cent of these individuals being male, the rest female. Table 21 below shows the number of offences.

Table 21   Exeter shoplifting: Previous offences of shoplifters (offender sample)

	1 previous offence	2 previous offences	3—10 previous offences	11 or more previous offences	Total
Males	4	–	5	5	14
Females	3	2	1	1	7

NOTE: These offences are not necessarily just for shoplifting, numbers were too small to justify greater division

Disposal of offenders

The caution is the most popular method for the very young and the very old, as Table 22 shows. Most shopkeepers and courts seem to feel that it is absurd to put a youngster through a court process and perhaps jeopardise his future career for the sake, say, of the theft of a 10p bar of chocolate. The survey showed that 44·6 per cent of all offenders were cautioned, while 33·8 per cent of offenders were fined, 7·6 per cent imprisoned and 13·8 per cent were otherwise dealt with.

Victim reaction

Given the size of the shoplifting problem it is interesting to consider how the victims react to this. Shopkeepers were asked whether or not they took any action to prevent shoplifting first of all, and their answers to this appear below in Table 23. Sixty per cent of counter-service shops felt that they had no need to take any action. Of all shops, 19·6 per cent took no action, and only 50 per cent of shops do take some action to prevent shoplifting. The 35 per cent of mixed-service shops who take no action perhaps reflects (as well as ignorance or despair) lack of a clear-cut perception of what kind of risk category they are in, and what sort of problem they face.

Table 22 Exeter shoplifting: Method of disposal of offenders (offender sample)

Age	Case Dismissed	Suspended Sentence	Imprisonment	Fine	Caution	Supervision order	Cautioned and left	Conditional discharge	Probation	Total
Up to 15	–	–	–	3	26	2	–	–	–	31
16–20	–	–	–	4	–	–	–	2	1	7
21–30	–	1	–	5	–	–	2	–	–	8
31–40	–	–	3	3	1	–	–	–	–	7
41–50	1	–	–	2	–	–	–	–	–	3
51–60	–	–	1	5	–	–	–	–	–	6
61 and over	–	–	1	–	2	–	–	–	–	3
Total	1	1	5	22	29	2	2	2	1	65

Table 23 *Exeter shoplifting: Action taken to prevent shoplifting (shopkeeper sample)*

	Self-service shops	Counter-service shops	Mixed-service shops	Total
Action taken	13	8	10	31
No action taken	3	3	6	12
No action needed	–	17	1	18
Total	16	28	17	61

One of the most obvious kinds of action possible is the employment of security staff. Not surprisingly, none of the mixed-service or counter-service shops did this. The salary for employing a detective is roughly £2,500 to £3,000 per annum. This means that it is only worth employing one when losses equal or exceed this salary figure. Of all shops, only 9·8 per cent did employ a detective, and only 37 per cent of self-service shops employ one. The obvious solution would be for more shops to share the services of detectives, yet very few do so, most preferring to have their own (who because she visits other branches too makes only rare appearances), or not bother.

For the victims, there is considerable uncertainty as to whether or not the police *should* be involved, or whether they should be deliberately excluded. Many confided that they do not bother to call the police in, because, as they said, if it goes as far as the court, 'the courts do nothing'.

The results on frequency with which the police are called in to deal with a shoplifter show that 26 per cent of shops in the sample never use the police. For self-service shops alone, the proportion is much higher (43·75 per cent). Only 22 per cent of shops always use the police, which indicates uncertainty as to whether shoplifting really is a crime or not in the minds of many shopkeepers. There is no similar doubt in people's minds when it comes to breaking and entering. A number of shopkeepers feel that a direct request for the shoplifter to pay for the goods and leave, or to put the goods down and leave, is the easiest way to deal with shoplifting. 'I take the bottle away from them, and tell them to go and not come back', 'I deal with a shoplifter so as not to cause embarrassment', 'I ask them if they would like to pay for the extra items', were typical comments. Yet again, others felt that physical assault without involving the police was the easiest way. 'If I catch them, I shake it out of them', as one said, or 'I administer the law myself, because the law is not doing its job. I caught one and bashed him in the face. I said, "Are you coming in here again?" He said, "No." I bashed him in the face again, and I let him go. He has not come back.' Yet again, 'Belt them, it upsets their dignity.' Such remarks, however, were not typical. One lady shopkeeper never contacted the police because she was frightened of threatened reprisals if she caught shoplifters and did so. Gangs had threatened that if she caught any of them they would smash her shop windows and set light to her outside oil fuel tank.

Recognition of shoplifters

Shopkeepers were asked whether or not they could recognise a shoplifter in action. In some ways this could be seen as a projective question, or loaded to produce an affirmative. However I do not think that this was the case, due to the presence of a built-in checking probe asking for details as to how recognition was achieved.

A total of 40·98 per cent of all shopkeepers claimed to be able to recognise a shoplifter. The proportion in self-service shops was 62·5 per cent. Few of those claiming ability to recognise seemed to be aware that recognition was dependent upon them being present at the time of the incident, and that it was in the interests of shoplifters in this game of 'keepers and takers' to pick a time when they were not. Fifty-nine per cent of all shopkeepers either could not recognise a shoplifter or did not know whether they could or not.

Those who claimed to be able to recognise a shoplifter were asked how this was done. Most frequently customers' actions or eye movements were given as answers to this. One said, 'if they [customers] are watching you, you watch them.' Another said that shoplifters always look at him and keep watching him. It was also frequently reported that shoplifters will quickly notice the presence of anti-shoplifting mirrors, and that it was easy to spot them doing that. Most agreed that the shoplifter 'looks' more than the legitimate shopper (as well as also acting suspiciously by moving furtively and so on). One said, 'they are glancing quickly all over the place, but if you stand still in front of them they won't see you'. Another said that those who are about to shoplift invariably (in his experience) drum their fingers restlessly on the display stand just before stealing.

Overall awareness of the problem

Counter-service shops were clearly aware of the protection against shoplifting that the counter and the serving of customers afforded. Many, too, felt little sympathy for the shoplifting problems of self-service shops; 'they are asking for it', and 'it is waiting to be picked up', were frequent comments about the high level of temptation offered in some self-service shops. One shopkeeper was extremely morally indignant about the temptation offered, amounting in his view to provocation. It was also pointed out that 'if you are working for yourself, you keep your eyes open', implying that the greater self-interest of the 'small man' in the counter-service shop conferred an immunity based upon self-interest which the impersonal service of the self-service shops did not have. Many of the larger self-service shop managers admitted that without self-service there would be little problem, accepting that strong temptation was present, and that self-service facilitates shoplifting, and accepting that it 'is natural' for people to take things if not actively stopped.

Such shops also pointed out that 'if you have not got it out, it won't sell', meaning that goods under glass counters do not sell as well as openly tempting display goods, and saying that they have to be self-service to compete. Shops that had recently converted to self-service were most aware of how rates of shoplifting had shot up dramatically since their change-over. It is interesting to see how in Table 24, many justifications are produced, supposed reasons for shoplifting, with very few mentions of the degree of provocation offered by supermarkets and the like.[6]

The low concern or interest of the relatively untroubled counter-service shops is apparent. The degree of temptation offered does not come through very well in these replies, and in the results to the question on how shoplifters should be dealt with, the degree of provocation, temptation or complicity in the production of crime is completely forgotten, and a frequent request was for 'tougher penalties', completely overlooking the earlier statements that sometimes self-service shops themselves were to blame for inducing crime.

Table 24 Exeter shoplifting: Opinions as to why people shoplift (shopkeeper sample)

Reason why	Self-service shops	Counter-service shops	Mixed-service shops	Total
Greed	3	2	1	6
Poverty	1	–	–	1
Boredom	1	1	–	2
Easy money, not seen as theft	2	1	4	7
'Illness'	–	–	1	1
Daredevilry	6	1	4	11
Temptation	1	2	3	6
Don't know	2	21	4	27
Total	16	28	17	61

When asked how shoplifters should be dealt with, 21 per cent of all shops expressed the view that the penalties for shoplifting should be 'tougher' (56 per cent of self-service shops felt this). As before, counter-service shops felt uninvolved and uninterested in what for them was largely other people's problems.

Shopkeepers were then asked for their views on how shoplifting might be stopped, and their response is listed below in Table 25. Results from this question show only that self-service shops have thought about the problem more, and have become more frustrated by it. It is of course especially interesting that in so many cases shopkeepers see it as the duty of others to protect them, without apparently realising the obstacles that many of them put in the path of the others who are trying to do this. It is similarly interesting the way in which self-service shops do not fully want to appreciate the extent to which counter service confers relative immunity. So that for many, the fact that shoplifting occurs is the fault of 'the family' or 'the police' and so on, rather than being anything to do with the way their own shop is arranged. One manager said, 'it is terrible to have

Table 25 Exeter shoplifting: How shoplifting might be stopped (shopkeeper sample)

Opinion as to how to stop	Self-Service shops	Counter-service shops	Mixed-service shops	Total
Closed circuit TV	–	–	1	1
Greater vigilance	1	–	1	2
Use of notices indicating intention of prosecuting	2	–	–	2
A family responsibility	1	2	1	4
Prosecute more often	–	–	1	1
Search customers on leaving	1	–	–	1
Discontinue self-service	1	–	–	1
Physically assault detected shoplifters	1	–	3	4
Tougher penalties awarded by courts	3	2	–	5
Impossible to stop shoplifters	5	–	4	9
Don't know	1	24	6	31
Total	16	28	17	61

to watch everybody, not to be able to trust anybody, it makes you twitch.' Yet this same informant argued that shoplifting was not criminal, saying, 'everybody does it.'

Theft by shop staff

The information obtained on theft by shop staff was not of particularly high quality. Several shopkeepers said that this was less of a problem now that staff were paid more than in the past, but at least a handful of shops felt this to be a menace of uncertain proportions. Certainly some of the supposed shoplifting offences by customers could scarcely be carried out without the connivance of assistants (for example, an instance that was reported of the theft of a circular saw from an ironmonger's).[7]

It was also clear with those shops employing store detectives that the detectives were there as much to check on the staff (with spot bag searches) as on the customers. It was pointed out that if an assistant is determined to steal, then it is impossible to stop him. Instances were quoted of an assistant 'saving up for her marriage' regularly taking money from her till, and concealing it in her shoe until she left the shop at night. In another shop, staff regularly hide money which they have stolen in the rubbish waiting to be collected in the backyard. As the manager said, 'I cannot be like a rat, and rummage through the rubbish every morning.' More commonly, there is little check, as was pointed out, on how often an assistant rings up 50p for a 75p sale and pockets the difference. One shop indicated a reluctance to involve the police in investigating theft by members of staff, saying that they were 'heavy-handed'. Eighteen per cent of all shops admitted that they had some theft by staff during the last year, and in self-service shops the figure was 37 per cent. Many shops simply did not know, or were reluctant to indicate.

For example, several women's clothes shop manageresses pointed out that when they come across an empty hanger for a dress, one of four things could have happened. It could be that the shop assistant has sold the dress and forgotten to mark the sale off, or that the dress has been shoplifted. Alternatively the dress might have been inexpertly stolen by a member of staff, or it could have been stolen by a shopper accomplice of a member of staff. Such an example points to the difficulties that shops have in estimating their losses and the origin of these.

Means of preventing shoplifting

It now seems possible to tentatively suggest that the main determinants of the amount of shoplifting a shop has are: (*a*) the type of good being sold, (*b*) sales policy, (*c*) availability of staff, (*d*) shop geography, (*e*) display features, (*f*) use of crime prevention devices.

The type of good being sold can function to exclude a great deal of shoplifting. Shops which sell only very large items (such as carpets) or very heavy items (such as machines) are less at risk than those which sell small, light items. (However, they may be more at risk to breaking and entering.) Shops which can sell goods of the unwrapped, untinned, unbagged kind (such as vegetables or meat) have less of a problem than do those selling pre-packed, wrapped goods. As one butcher said, explaining his absence of a shoplifting problem, 'you can't walk down the street with a piece of raw meat in your hand, now, can you?' Some shops, too, can arrange the goods that they are selling so as to make shoplifting very difficult, if not impossible. Record shops can keep their records and cassettes behind the counter, and leave only the sleeves in front for the customers to select from (in such a shop, however, empty sleeves were still being stolen). Shoe shops can put only one of a pair of shoes on display, rather than both, although it was pointed out that even then occasionally people will steal two odd shoes and go to another branch of the same firm saying, 'I must have been given these by mistake, can you pair them?'

The sales policy of the shop is the second principal determinant of the amount of shoplifting that any shop will experience. If a shop has a self-service sales policy, then it will sell its goods fast, because customers can see them and handle them easily. It will also operate cheaply and quickly, because less staff are needed (just 'ringers' at the check-out counters), and they will take less time to serve each customer, largely because they are not offering anything in the way of advice, information, service, helpfulness, sympathy, or anything but the facility of taking the customers' money with indifference. Such self-service shops are popular, because of their novelty, their range of goods, all of which can be purchased in one place, and the apparent cheapness of some lines. This means that they are crowded and busy, as well as having relatively few assistants. Self-service shops with fewer assistants to the square metre and bigger and better delights than in other shops are also anonymous because of their busyness, and there is more space and 'cover' for the would-be shoplifter to 'stalk' the assistant. It is also legitimate to be seen handling the goods, which would facilitate theft. Shops with such a sales policy must accept high shoplifting losses, although they usually have no idea of what these losses are precisely, since they have so many other sorts of losses to contend with such as short-delivery at the door by van-men, theft by shop assistants and so on.

Shops which have a counter-service sales policy have a much slower turnover of goods, and rely much less on impulse buying. They do not sell so fast, and their shop is not as consistently filled, but they will usually accept this, since they are usually in lines where people have to come to them sooner or later, and could scarcely be persuaded to buy on impulse anyway. In counter-service shops, great reliance is put on 'staff' and on the idea of 'service' meaning kindly, informing interest, and it is accepted that it is this 'service' which results in a sale, rather than the ready proximity of the good as in the self-service shop which enables the customer to snatch it and take it to the till. Most goods in counter-service shops are under glass counters, in boxes, or in cupboards, or display cases, and it is the assistant who brings them to the customer. Clearly in such shops each sale takes longer than in a self-service shop, and more staff will be needed. The very fact that large quantities of staff are available and that they are anxious to help a customer means that shoplifters find counter-service shops unsatisfactory places to work in.

Availability of staff is the third determinant of amount of shoplifting. If shops wish to economise on staff, then they can expect more shoplifting, but if they can keep a reasonably high density of staff cover and maintain that at all times throughout the day, then much less shoplifting will occur because of staff presence (that is, irrespective of their vigilance). If at the same time the staff are also known and trusted, and vigilant, then the amount of shoplifting (and of course staff theft) that occurs will be slight. It tends to be the case that in self-service shops relatively few staff are available at any given time during the day, and that at some times (for example lunch-time) the number available is even more drastically reduced by staff having meals or breaks. Assistants in self-service shops also perhaps tend to be both less vigilant and trustworthy than assistants in counter-service shops, because there is a faster staff turnover (which means that staff are an unknown quantity), and because there is more impersonality, more alienation in such work, there is less sense of commitment (and loyalty) by the assistant to the shop by and large.

The 'geography' of a shop is important from the shoplifting point of view too; if the shop is set back a long way from the road with only one entrance and exit this discourages shoplifters, who prefer a shop fronting on to a busy street with plenty of entrances for a quick, smooth escape. The shop should have good unobstructed vision within it, and tills and counters should be set up with good fields of vision. Those shops which have more than four sides, and many alcoves and nooks as well as substantial supporting pillars appearing at intervals and recesses, provide 'cover' for the shoplifter which the assistant's eye cannot penetrate. The simplest and most effective design is the square shop with the door at one end, and the counter across the other, giving a good clear view of customers.

There are many display features which will function to increase or reduce the amount of shoplifting, and much can be done here to reduce the amount of shoplifting that can possibly occur in a shop. Below is a list of display features which shopkeepers have mentioned as critical in relation to shoplifting.

1. Shoplifters will not steal from the top floor of a shop or the back of it so readily as from the ground floor, particularly at the front near the door.
2. From this it follows that 'high-risk' items should be kept at the rear of the shop near the office, and that
3. No small items should be kept near the door, where a hand can reach in and grab them.
4. Moving the goods around in a shop boosts sales as is well known, since people 'discover' other wanted goods while hunting for what they originally wanted. What is less well known is that moving goods around also helps to foil premeditated shoplifting based upon the shoplifter knowing where the goods are.
5. Low display stands are crucial to reduce shoplifting. If they are low enough, they can be seen over by the assistant (who still cannot see people putting objects in their pockets, though), and they do not interfere with the vision principle mentioned earlier. High display stands mean that shoplifters will 'stalk' the assistants to their own advantage, using the piles of goods as 'cover' for their activities.

6. It is preferable to keep nothing which is of very high value on display at all (as jewellers have realised since medieval times).
7. A counter-service shop should avoid the use of open shelves or displays.
8. Where practicable, lockable glass showcases which make a noise when being opened (so that illicit opening can be heard) are preferable to the use of open shelf displays for small high-value items.

The final determinant of volume is the extent to which crime prevention devices are used. Some of those in common use are:

1. Store detectives. For most stores, detectives are prohibitively expensive, and are frequently disliked by staff because of the implication that they are being checked on too. Detectives are of most value if they can be on the shop-floor for long hours. The touring company detective who visits all branches of the firm means low hours of local cover. Sharing schemes, where a group of shops club together to share the services of a detective, seem more economically feasible, and mean that each shop has more cover hours.
2. Communication systems. Large, vulnerable stores often club together to form a network, each member of which will inform others by telephone of the activities of shoplifters in the area. Such an early warning system is usually a same-day operation, and is particularly useful against highly mobile professional gangs.
3. Alarms. Used for showcases, and doors and windows at night, most useful as a defence against breaking and entering.
4. Notices. Many shops are reluctant to risk insulting their customers by using a notice such as 'Shoplifters will be prosecuted', although most supermarkets have this type. 'Shoplifting is stealing' as a notice is perhaps as effective, with its tacit appeal to honesty and hidden implication of prosecution. Notices about the existence of store detectives, such as 'Store detectives in operation', are also useful.
5. Mirrors. These can be strip type on walls, pillars or ceilings, or circular type to focus on a corner or alcove. Display cases also of course frequently function in the same way that mirrors do.
6. Observation windows. One judiciously placed observation window with a good field of vision can be of special use in single-

person shops, to enable a shopkeeper doing accounts to scan his shop with a glance from his office. Such windows can be fitted with clear glass or one-way mirrors of course. 'Pill-box' type slits are also widely used with advantage in supermarkets, set high up in the side or rear wall.
7. Other measures. Closed-circuit television has been shown to be only a short-term deterrent with a short 'life', since day-long scanning is costly and shoplifters soon learn to ignore the threat it presents. Lockable glass backs to shop windows and wire grills (especially near the doorway) may be of use in some types of shop. In addition, chains can be used for high-value goods, such as power tools or radios, which can be chained and then padlocked together to make theft more difficult. With clothes shops, restricting the number of garments that can be taken into the fitting room to two or three is useful, as are communal fitting rooms, which not only prevent a shoplifter from 'wearing clothes out' or concealing them about her person, but are also shown to do away with 'ticket switching', where the cheap ticket taken from a cheap item replaces the expensive ticket on an expensive item.

Various other shop-specific measures have been developed by shopkeepers, who show great ingenuity in devising electrical or electronic detection equipment to suit their own purposes. (One informant, for example, repeatedly pestered by one particular shoplifter, who had been trying with varying degrees of success to steal transistor radios from his shop without so far having been caught, constructed a make-and-break circuit with a contact pad under each of the most vulnerable radios, so that if any of them were lifted the circuit was completed and a red light would show on a control panel hidden in a rear store-room.) Large self-service shops in some branches (but not in the Exeter area) have now started using a 'bag checkout', where customers can leave their bags while shopping in the charge of a cloakroom attendant, to reduce the opportunity of concealing unpaid for items in the shopping bag.

The use of such prevention devices, however, although it may function to help with the shoplifting problem, either substantially or for a time, is less important than the other major determinants that have been mentioned, i.e. type of good sold, policy, staff issues, and geography especially.

This concludes the summary of results from the survey in the Exeter area, which is of course one-sided in that more information has been obtained on victims than on offenders. As was mentioned above when discussing aims and objectives of the study, this was intentional, since previously virtually no information has been assembled on the victims of shoplifting and the extent to which their behaviour may inhibit or precipitate the offence. Nor has any study been made of the possible techniques of shoplifting control derived from the experience of shopkeepers themselves. In the following chapter I have tried to present general conclusions on the findings which have been acquired in relation to these topics, specifically discussing the role of the victim in relation to the crime of shoplifting, and basic premises of shoplifting control extrapolated from the study.

4
Conclusions

Care is needed in interpreting the results from the field study, since the Exeter area may constitute a 'special case' from the point of view of the crime of shoplifting. Self-evidently the results obtained would have been different if the study had been carried out on a nationwide basis. However, we can be reasonably certain that, although the study of the crime of shoplifting *was* only carried out in one area, this area is not that 'special' in terms of the amount or type of shoplifting present. In large conurbations, of course, rates of this type of theft would be higher (chiefly as a result of population at risk and numbers of available attractions), but there are good grounds for thinking that the direction of the error arising in a study of one county town such as this one tends to be solely towards an underestimate of the extent of the shoplifting that occurs. Had the investigation taken place in a larger urban area the results would have indicated far more shoplifting, but we cannot be at all sure that although in a larger area the results would have been different, that they would have differed on the basis of anything other than scale alone.

There is every reason to suppose that in the Exeter area shoplifting as a crime form only differs in size terms rather than in form terms from shoplifting in any other areas of the country, and this would continue to apply unless we were absolutely certain that in the Exeter region the population at risk was especially prone to shoplifting, or especially averse to it. There seem to be no grounds for this certainty.

The survey showed that in the Exeter area, shoplifting is extensively practised by large numbers of people. Conceivably shoplifting in this area is less large scale and less well organised than in other areas, although it was not the intention of this study to collect information on this issue.[1] In fact the only areas of the city with negligible incidence are those with virtually no shops. The greatest concentration of shoplifting is found in two long streets in the city centre, in all about half a mile in length, which contain the larger self-service shops chiefly as well as big department stores and popular chain stores. This area as a whole in 1975 attracted more than 80 per cent of the detected cases of shoplifting.

Detected offenders, by no means representative of all, show a scatter of age and occupation, with a large concentration of youthful thieves. This is rather disturbing in several ways; first, given biases of an inevitable kind in reporting offences, there is reason to hypothesise homogeneity of offenders in some way, and since this was not found it can only be supposed that shoplifting *is* extremely widespread and popular as a crime-form. Second, the high numbers of juvenile thieves augurs badly for the future, suggesting that little is functioning to inhibit children from stealing.

Rarely do detected offenders use any special techniques for their thefts, most of which are committed by an individual alone. It may be here of course that special method is largely confined to undetected offenders, who escape detection because of their *modus operandi*. In Exeter this seems relatively unlikely, however.

There is no evidence to show that shoplifting is other than extremely widespread. People shoplift for luxury-type goods, most frequently for themselves. For some it is an 'occupation', for others a 'game', for yet others a 'compulsion', or again 'morally justifiable', and as one informant said, 'some people want everything they can see'. Apparently shop theft has emerged out of abundance and plenty as a 'morality free' area for many, which is widely attractive to widely different groups of people.

No shop has a clear idea of how much it is losing through shoplifting. Shoplifting appears to be largely victim-precipitated in self-service shops (as some self-service and many counter-service shops indicated). The means of frustrating shoplifting as a crime-form already exists, that is the counter-service shop with plentiful staff serving customers. Self-service shops have learnt to adjust to a high level of shoplifting, since it is matched by an even higher sales curve. Counter-service shops have little or no problem with it, and are uninterested in it as a result, tending to blame self-service shops for its existence. The type of shop most affected and disturbed by shoplifting is the mixed-service type, where there is neither a clear self-service nor counter-service policy, nor are there sufficient staff to cope with the new problem created by the tentative, experimental drift from counter service to semi-self-service. Typically, the small shop with a semi-self-service conversion recently installed is hard hit.

Stripped of the protection offered by counter service (of which it may not have been fully aware), it does not have a large enough financial backing to afford big losses like large self-service shops who write off shoplifting as a 'stock-loss', nor does it have enough staff who are fully aware of the problem, and soon the manager finds that he does not really know what he has started to involve himself with, as he is gradually withdrawn by economic forces from the predictable, stable world with which he was familiar. Such mixed-service shops without a clear conception of who they are (what type of shop) and what they are doing (what their sales policy should be, and what sort of entrepreneurial risks they are running) are most disrupted by shoplifting. The large self-service shop is prepared to pay the price of high rates of shoplifting for greater sales, the counter-service shop would rather have the security than the higher sales (plus built-in theft factor). The mixed-service shop remains in the middle, indecisive, and getting the worst of both worlds, with relatively low sales, and relatively high shoplifting rates for its size.

It is now possible to reconsider the original hypotheses in the light of the field evidence. Conclusions on these are presented below.

1. *Shops with counter service will have less shoplifting than self-service shops.*

To test this, information on the estimated extent of shoplifting, obtained from the shopkeeper sample, was crossed with the type of sales policy in operation. The hypothesis is, in fact, upheld at better than the ·001 level of probability. Counter-service shops do have significantly less shoplifting than self-service ones. This hypothesis can be accepted on this evidence, but as well as this, various other sorts of information collected favour accepting it. In the survey shopkeepers were asked, for example, for the date when they last had a case of shoplifting in their shop. For the counter-service group of shops in the sample, 32 per cent could not recall having a case at all, whereas every self-service shop in the sample had had cases. Again, 3 per cent of the counter-service shops had had a case within the week preceding the survey, and 56 per cent of the self-service shops had had at least one known case in the last week. This seems to be further evidence favouring the acceptance of the hypothesis. A factor superficially militating against this is the number of cases known to the police occurring in particular shop types. This information showed that 26 per cent of all cases of shoplifting in the area occurred in small, counter-service shops, and 44 per cent of cases occurred in shops that were predominantly self-service. However, in interpreting this type of information, preparedness to involve the police in a case is a separate influencing factor.

2. *The larger the shop, the more the shoplifting.*
A larger shop of course requires more overseeing to protect it from shoplifters, and it also, in turn, requires more staff. If the shop is not permanently staffed throughout opening hours in a realistic and appropriate way with experienced, alert, motivated assistants, this makes the task of the shoplifter easier, whether he is the amateur shoplifter described by Gibbons (1968) or the professional. A further complication arises in that the more staff involved, the greater the likelihood of staff dishonesty evidencing itself, purely on a statistical basis, or lack of interest and sense of involvement on the part of the staff. The man running the small shop has far greater control, control over his assistants, over his stock, and over his shop-floor. He has a slower turnover, but he also has more customers who are personally known to him, and more clearly defined shopping norms, both of which would operate in his favour with regard to the level of shoplifting which he experiences. To test this hypothesis, shop size was compared with estimated extent of shoplifting information (given by the shopkeeper sample). This showed that the hypothesis must be rejected, that there is no evidence to accept that shop *size* alone is a critical variable.

3. *Shops occupying sites in city centres are more likely to suffer from shoplifters than shops in outlying areas.*
The area distribution of known shoplifting offences reveals that 80 per cent of shoplifting cases occurred in the city centre area (the High Street zone), where there are in any case more shops. Outlying areas of course anyway tend to contain less shops. This seems to argue in favour of accepting the hypothesis. However, using data from the shopkeeper sample, the relationship between locality and

amount of shoplifting was not statistically significant. Hence this hypothesis must be rejected.

4. *Shops selling luxuries are more likely to suffer more from shoplifters than those selling necessities.*

Data from the offender sample showed fairly clearly that food, cosmetics and clothing are extremely popular choices of goods from the shoplifter's point of view. Shop-owners and managers were adamant that goods most frequently selected were of the luxury type, irrespective of the type of shop that they were running. It is of course quite possible that in so far as luxuries tend to be priced higher than other goods, shopkeepers keep a closer check on their stocks of these, and hence *notice* more theft of luxuries than of necessities. Certainly, at the impressionistic level, shops concentrating on the sale of luxuries alone tended to have a more pronounced shoplifting problem. (However, increasing lack of specialisation in selling, to maximise profit, makes it harder to check on this sort of thing.) Generally the evidence collected falsifies this hypothesis. No significant difference was found between shops selling luxuries and necessities in respect of the amount of shoplifting experienced.

5. *Shops that have high rates of shoplifting will tend to blame outside agencies for this.*

Overall, 21 per cent of all shops in the sample expressed the view that there should be harsher penalties for shoplifters, and significantly, the percentage for self-service shops alone (given the high level of theft which they face) was 56 per cent. Counter-service shop-owners tended to blame supermarkets and department stores for encouraging shoplifting. Shops with high rates of theft certainly had thought about the problem much more, as was to be expected, and showed a wider scatter of suggestions for curbing the rise in shoplifting than counter-service shops. Many shop-owners in high-risk shops were extremely contemptuous of the legal process and its effect and coverage, and of the public, and only one in the high-risk category accepted that allowing people to handle goods in a 'help-yourself' atmosphere would be much more likely to increase level of theft. For the majority, there was a complacent smugness about sales policy, and a great deal of indignant outraged statements about customary behaviour of customers and lack of support from the law courts. Although this kind of information appears to support the hypothesis, we must conclude that insufficient information was forthcoming to provide a real test for this hypothesis.

6. *The more heterogeneous the clientele in any one shop, the more shoplifting is likely to occur.*

Regrettably, on the evidence collected it was not possible to test this hypothesis.

Some final remarks are called for about the attitudes of the shopkeepers with a wide experience of shoplifting as a daily event, mostly managers of self-service shops. One of the informants said, 'it is not our job to stop shoplifting, we are not social workers.' Such shopkeepers regard shoplifting cases as tiresome incidents with no known cause, which disturb the smooth running of their main concern, their business, something external which is imposed upon them from outside. They are of course in business for business's sake, and as the Duke of Wellington said, 'Call on a businessman only at business times, and on business; transact your business, and go about your business, in order to give him time to finish his business.'

Shopkeepers do not justifiably see themselves as custodians of morality. As far as they are concerned, shoplifting is a small, irritating part of 'shrinkage', which they can allow for in an economic sense.[2] Shopkeepers do not see stopping shoplifting as their 'business', they see it as other people's business, the business of the family, the police or the court. Some of them may miss the obvious, that the pursuit of such a self-interested view, ultimately and paradoxically, does not lead to the furtherance of self-interest. Short of some drastic (and improbable) change in the rearing of the nation's children, it is shopkeepers alone who hold in their hands the means of preventing shoplifting, through changing their sales policies, in fact through restricting their greed, and this is especially the case with so-called supermarkets.

What is a small and usually insignificant problem for the shopkeeper, a case of shoplifting, becomes magnified in impact and cost, both to the shoplifter and to the community, the further away the case is removed from the shop venue. At the worst, a trifling theft from a shop will involve the time and trouble of a police investigation, time and money spent in law courts, possibly the cost of lodging in prison, and social workers' time. In cost terms, both financial and emotional, there is a funnelling outwards from the point of origin (the actual theft), which becomes on a large scale, multiplied by thousands of cases, a crippling burden to the community. Shopkeepers however do not see it this way, because they are usually unaware of the amount of administration, paperwork, and time and effort and travel which one case of shoplifting can generate.

The owner of the large supermarket responds to the general high level of shoplifting in his shop, because it is encapsulated inside the shrinkage figure, with moral indifference, and he has a variety of ways of explaining this, saying that there will always be shoplifting, or that only a few people are involved, or that his shop is in a special position with regard to shoplifting. On the other hand, cases of shoplifting which refuse to remain concealed and camouflaged in the shrinkage figure arouse his ire and moral indignation. To this he responds by asking, what are the police doing? Or, why can he not have the protection from shoplifters which the presence of a police force is supposed to confer?

Shoplifting in general he can be indifferent to, but particular cases that come to his attention arouse great indignation, as he becomes exasperated by the blatant boldness of organised thieves. It appears to be the case that such shopkeepers are enveloped in moral inconsistency, and are unable to realise or accept that tempting and provoking help-yourself shops where customers are allowed to handle goods freely do in fact generate greater rates of shoplifting, and that this has nothing to do with police inefficiency, or the actions of law courts, but has a very great deal to do with the immediate availability of goods in a morally unstructured social environment.

It is of course easy enough for such shopkeepers to hold up their hands in horror, and ask for greater protection, and to turn to the community and ask for greater morality. This is acceptable, but impractical, for reasons mentioned above, since greater protection cannot be offered (or if it actually was, it would not be accepted) and greater morality cannot be obtained merely by asking for it because of a sense of injustice. What is practical, and what can be obtained, is to change the format of shops to preclude impulse purchase (which is, if morality is going to be invoked in the argument, of very questionable morality itself).

However, such shopkeepers are so preoccupied with managing

their own moral inconsistency that they find it difficult to break out from the trite, circular, interrogative verbal defences which they use to mask this, and they cannot see the obvious, that the solution is largely in their hands. There can be no suggestion that shoplifting can be eradicated completely, that it could ever be made to vanish. More to the point, does our community have to tolerate such a high rate, and the concomitant social and economic costs of having such a rate? This might be something which we would *have* to endure, if there were not already at hand a solution. This argument suggests that the solution has been missed, because of the way in which some shopkeepers attempt to resolve the dilemma of their moral inconsistency, and that the rest of the community is paying a very high price for this self-indulgence on the part of a minority of shopkeepers of large, self-service combines.

Returning to the main argument, the general conclusions which we can draw from this study are that:

1. Shoplifting is an enduring crime with a high survival rate, manifesting extensive resistance to pressures to control it. It is doubtful if increased security in the form of technical devices achieves anything more than a temporary reduction in the problem.
2. In counter-service shops, the rate of shoplifting is negligible.
3. In self-service shops, the rate of shoplifting is high.
4. Apparently the part played by the potential victim in the crime of shoplifting is important. Through examining victim behaviour in shoplifting, we do get an insight into this crime and its dimensions.

Revising and developing the rather determinist framework produced in Chapter 2, in the section 'Nine questions for the shoplifter', it is possible to quickly flow chart the various constraints which the shoplifter is confronted with. Figure 1 is an example of how this could now appear.

Starting at the top of the chart, the first decision that confronts the shoplifter is whether the goal is available. In practical terms, this means querying whether the shops are accessible to him and open. Second, the shoplifter requires time to commit his crime, and by 'empty time' is meant time when he is not accountable to others who might disapprove of his act, or frustrate it, or simply require him to be elsewhere engaged in another activity. So leisure is required. Third, the particular shop which the shoplifter has in mind for a

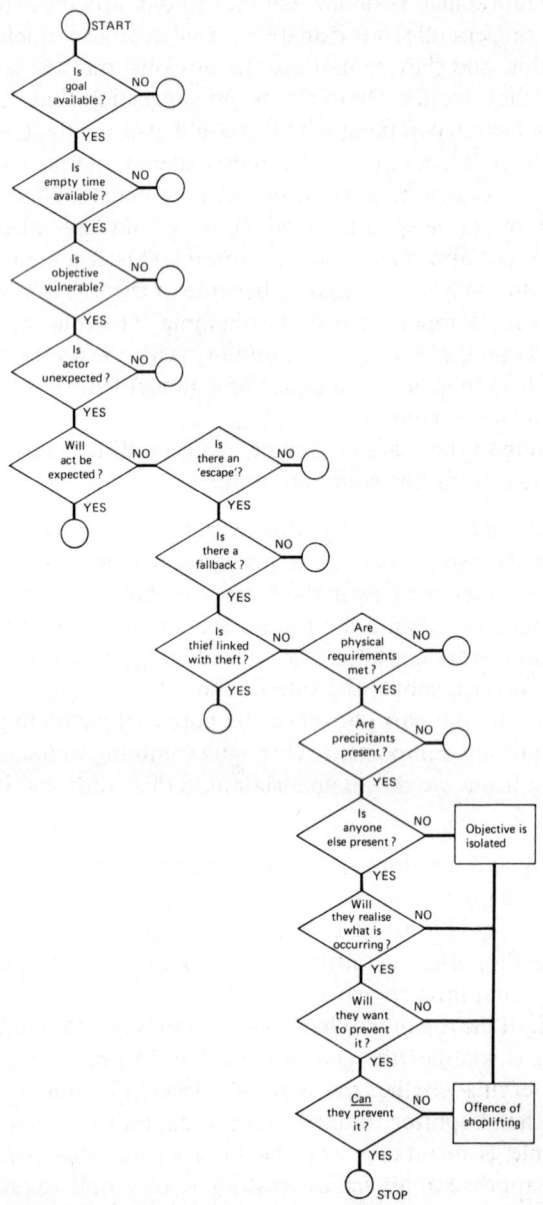

Figure 1 Constraints in the crime of shoplifting

Conclusions 99

target should be vulnerable to shoplifting in various ways before the shoplifter would consider stealing. Fourth, the shoplifter must feel that he does not appear like an obvious thief. He must feel that no one would suspect him of shoplifting, and he has to be sure that when he actually steals the act of theft itself will be unexpected in this particular shop.

Further, he requires a foolproof means of escaping rapidly from the shop once he has stolen, and a fall-back or alternative escape avenue if his first choice is blocked for some reason. The shoplifter's eighth check before stealing is to assess whether or not there is anything which would link him to the theft after it has occurred. If, in his judgement, there is not, then he must consider whether the physical requirements of the crime are satisfactorily met in this particular shop, which will probably relate specifically to elements such as privacy and opportunity for concealment of goods. Some idiosyncratic precipitant is required before the act can occur. The shoplifter must have his own reason for stealing and a trigger for this particular theft. Finally, just before stealing, he must ask himself four particular questions concerning the number, location and expected vigilance of shop staff and customers. If, in his own estimate, he can get satisfactory answers to each of the questions listed in the chart, then, the argument is, shoplifting will occur regardless.

The whole chart represented in Figure 1 is predicated upon two key features. First, it attempts to portray the crime of shoplifting from the shoplifter's *own subjective viewpoint*. In taking decisions prior to the act of theft, what matters is not the objective state of affairs extant in a particular shop, but the potential shoplifter's subjective estimate of them. Second, there is an assumption of rationality, of purposive behaviour on the part of the shoplifter. There is of course no suggestion that shoplifters stand at the shop-door, and ask themselves a string of questions in a set order before committing themselves to stealing. Very often, particularly with habitual shoplifters who have developed a feel for the process as a result of great practice, there is every reason to suppose that the assessment about viability will be almost unconscious, intuitive and rapid, but none the less rational. This assumption of rationality can be criticised in at least two main ways. It can be argued that shoplifters who were mentally ill would not operate in this way at all, and second, that in such a presentation, no account is taken of the role of chance or impulse in shoplifting by nimble-fingered opportunists. Both of these objections must stand.

However, the point in such a chart is not to try and cover every conceivable set of circumstances, but to highlight crucial constraints which affect the success or failure of the shoplifter in attaining his target. Such a chart indicates three important features in relation to shoplifting. It demonstrates first that locating an opportunity to steal is not easy for the shoplifter. It would in fact be quite rare for all these listed conditions to be met in their optimum form in a real-life situation (high levels of observed theft indicate that they are usually not). It is, however, possible, even given these constraints, for the dice to be loaded in favour of the shoplifter, and for him to put together the right combination to ensure that this happens as often as possible. The argument is that this is precisely what occurs in the self-service shop, but happens much more rarely in the counter-service shop, where many more 'blocks' can be expected and located in the flow chart. Third, such a flow chart illustrates the nature of the interaction between criminal, criminal event and victim, forcing us to appreciate yet again that if one of these components is removed, crime does not occur.

We could easily rewrite this flow chart derived from the offence of shoplifting into a second experimental format, with perhaps wider applicability to other types of theft. To do this would involve some additions and alterations, but the same conditions and the same criticisms would still apply. The limitations of such a procedure are obvious, so are the advantages; the boundaries of the problem are isolated, and we are invited to focus upon them, so that the problem is more sharply defined; the innate complexity of the process is revealed, especially the quantity of constraints; and the role of the victim is highlighted.

Expanding the argument presented in Figure 1 gives the following run-down to the offence of theft. For a crime to occur, first the victim or the goal must be present and accessible, and must present themselves to the criminal so that they can be seen as such. The victim must be isolatable (even though, perhaps, present in a crowd), and available. A crime will not happen if a victim is not present, self-evidently, or if there is no suitable criminal objective which is exploitable.

As well as being available and present, the victim or goal must be vulnerable, preferably unprotected. (The burglar finds his task easier if there is no burglar alarm.) If the victim or goal is defended or fortified in some way, for the crime to occur the criminal must possess knowledge of means to neutralise the efficacy of protection or resistance. The criminal must know how to defuse a potentially explosive situation through, for example, disarming words or sympathetic non-verbal communication (or merely know how to dismantle a burglar alarm).

To engage in crime at all, the criminal must have free time. That is, time when he is unsupervised and unguided by others. He must not be expected anywhere else, or required by anyone else to do anything else, at the time when he wishes to commit the crime. Temporarily he must not be accountable to others, and he must be able to return to a non-criminal situation without having to account for his actions or absence, except superficially. He needs to be a temporary free agent, free to move as he pleases. If this condition cannot be met then almost certainly it will be made the harder for him to commit crime. He needs 'empty time'.

The venue for the crime-to-be should be unexpected, unlikely, and not normally associated in the mind of the victim with the type of event which the criminal has in mind. This would represent the ideal, not always attainable. (Bank cashiers *do* expect robbery to occur in the bank, but not all the time, and not at all at their home.) For the criminal it is much easier to do the act if at that particular time in that particular place the intended victim is not expecting a crime to occur. People may expect crimes to occur in some particular places and adjust their level of vigilance accordingly, in order to avoid attaining the victim status. This would be at variance with the requirements of the criminal, who needs an unsuspecting victim.

The criminal-to-be should not appear like a criminal in the eyes of the potential victim, and his arrival or action should be totally unexpected. Few victims have previous experience of how criminals do appear. However, newspapers, films and television portray the criminal in such a convincing way that the victim-to-be feels that he *has* met criminals before and knows what they look like, and how they behave before and during the crime. Films and television, through clever camera work, aim to ensure that the audience in advance of the theatrical crime is aware that the criminal is a criminal, whatever the other screen characters think of him. He may be presented as an 'obvious' criminal, via an 'insight' into his character, actions or morality, produced by a film clip such as a 'flashback' into his past.

All of this operates to the criminal's advantage, since it ensures that the would-be victim feels that he knows who real criminals are, and that he could always identify them in real life if need be, in advance of their actions, in the same way that he does from the safety of the cinema seat. This media-induced smugness about identification means that to escape amateur detection all the real criminal has to do not to be encoded in the victim's mind as a criminal is not to appear as criminals do on the films. This way he protects his 'unexpectedness', which can be revealed at his leisure. The nature of the criminal act must be unexpected; only in this way is it likely to be successful. For as long as possible the criminal must conceal his intentions as to precisely what he is about to do. If the *act* is unexpected, then the victim-to-be is caught unawares, with defences down, and has a low level of vigilance to match this. The criminal must be sure that no 'warning' of future intent is given to the intended victim, through either words or actions. The crime then comes as a total surprise, with all that that implies in terms of the inability of the victim to control the developing situation.

The criminal needs an 'escape' from the crime, that is a technique of withdrawal. This may be physical (such as a door or window which has been deliberately left open in advance to provide an escape route), or verbal (such as a ready excuse if unexpected intrusion or interruption takes place).

As well as the 'escape', the criminal also requires a 'fall-back', which is an alternative escape route which he can use, if blocked in his use of the first one for some reason. Again, the fall-back can be either physical or verbal. It may be yet another way out from the building the criminal is in, or it may be a verbal fall-back such as saying to the intended victim 'you didn't think I really meant it, did you ?', if the victim has realised the criminal's likely intention, and has now increased his level of watchfulness and suspicion because of this to a point where to successfully complete the crime no longer becomes possible from the criminal's point of view.

It is important to the criminal that the scene of the crime provides no immediate way in which the crime will be *linked* to him. There is a better chance of this condition being met if the criminal act takes place in an area where the criminal is unknown or where his presence is unexpected, or where it is difficult to establish that he was in fact present. For the criminal, there must be as few links as possible between him and the act which he is about to commit.

The intended *place* for the commission of the crime must meet the physical requirements necessary for the performance of the act. Depending upon the crime envisaged, the place where it is to occur must be dark and lonely, or alternatively it may need to be well-lit and crowded. At the same time the *means* to bring the crime to a successful conclusion must be present there, if there are any such special requirements (which usually with shoplifting there are not). It may be that the necessary implements are readily available in the environs (such as a garden spade left in a tool-shed, which can be used to break open a door), if not, then they will have to have been transported there in advance by the criminal. The criminal may need to bring with him gloves, thermic lances and gas bottles or similar articles.

Precipitating factors to trigger the crime need to be present. This includes obviously the whole area of motive, as well as immediate temptations and pressures to commit the crime (such as the presence and use of alcohol, or tiredness, provocation, teasing, taunting etc.).

Finally, for any type of crime, a set number of other people must be present apart from the criminal or criminals. Usually, from the criminal's point of view, it is most desirable for him to be alone with the victim or goal, without fear of interruptions. (Perhaps an empty room is required providing privacy, or certain knowledge that other people are not due back until a certain time.) Three other forms of interaction in the prodromal criminal situation also fail to inhibit crime commission. Form two is where, apart from the criminal and the victim, other people are present, but the criminal's assessment of the situation is that none of them will realise what is about to occur or occurring, and hence will not intervene. This might happen through onlookers' vision being temporarily (and perhaps deliberately) restricted, or through ignorance of the appearance of a crime. This is the most likely situation to be encountered in the crime of shoplifting.

Form three would be where other people are present apart from the criminal and victim or goal, but they do not wish to prevent the crime from occurring. If anything, they may even actually want it to, arising, for example, as a result of complicity or intimidation.

Form four is where others are present, but none of them *can* prevent what is about to occur. A bank robbery would be an example, where in the face of a determined and planned act, ruthlessly executed, onlookers are lacking in the necessary vigilance, speed and power to efficiently combat it.

Each type of crime, whether a burglary or a robbery, has attached to it its most appropriate number of victims, onlookers, bystanders, witnesses and observers. (Burglars prefer privacy, pickpockets prefer a crowd, and robbers can tolerate bystanders, because they feel confident in their ability to overcome any resistance from them.) With any one of these four forms, crime can occur.

This revised and expanded model of the constraints that surround theft targets is shown in Figure 2 below, and it is tentatively suggested that we might be able to use this to map all crimes of theft, not just shoplifting, recalling that if subjective estimates of the ease with which a constraint can be countered are unfavourable as the criminal sees it, crime will not ensue. Adequate ratings in relation to each of these issues (drawn as decision diamonds and event boxes) must be obtained before the criminal will operate with confidence. A rearrangement of the highly complex, dynamic and interlocking pattern produced by a changed constraint or an unfavourable estimate will function to block the particular putative theft in question from occurring.

Examining these models in relation to shoplifting again suggests no reasons why the crime should remain static in level, or diminish, given the structure of opportunity offered by current sales practices.

It is very easy to criticise the two models which have been put forward to describe the background to the theft process at the scene of the crime. However, such 'scene of crime' analysis does have the merit that it draws attention to ways in which victims can leave gates open for criminals (without of course specifying why, or how many people will take advantage of this).

Interpretations of crime relying upon evidence concerning availability and opportunity do not constitute explanations of crime, of course, but they do indicate how wide is the neck of the bottle through which all crime must pass, whatever its aetiology. They may also suggest some rather obvious prevention techniques, ways of restricting opportunity and reducing ready availability. None of this perhaps should be discussed in isolation from the population at risk and its motivations for committing the crime in

Conclusions 105

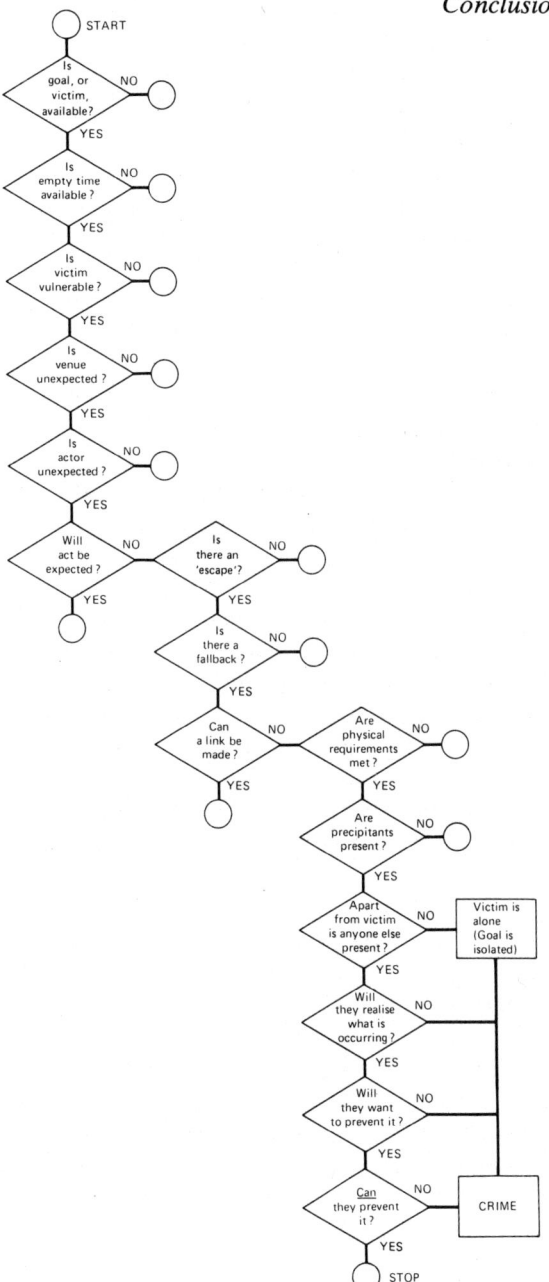

Figure 2 Constraints in crimes of theft

question, but customarily the lure of looking at this population means that some very obvious features of victim-situation and how the scene of the crime presents itself to the criminal can easily be neglected. The argument is that crime may be prevented more easily by changing the format of the arena within which it might occur, and by changing victim behaviour, rather than through a more and more intensive scrutiny of the people who commit it.

The study as a whole has been undertaken as a test of how useful this approach might be for theft in general. Perhaps it is possible that through thinking in this way about particular crime-forms, some ideas for activating latent, internal, crime-regulating factors which can function independently of the police and the law may be generated. A popular alternative, that we accept that crime occurs independently of victims' actions and the perceived structure of the pre-crime location, is unthinkable, in so far as it places the burden for the control of all theft exclusively in the hands of the already overworked police and courts, and at the same time holds out no immediate hope for any diminution in the crime in question. Such a view quickly crystallises into acceptance of what is apparently the easiest way of controlling crime, through increasing legal sanctions and controls. The suggestion here is that scene-of-crime analysis and consideration of the victim's situation quickly by-passes such circularity and furthermore offers more positive means of grappling with the problem, with the raw materials at hand, rather than asking for more and more of external, scarce resources, such as police time.

Reverting to the specifics of shoplifting, and summarising what has been collected so far on the prevention of it, it is possible to produce a worksheet of practical shoplifting prevention points. It is not suggested that following these points will remove the problem, but they may help the individual shopkeeper to organise his resistance to it more efficiently. In large part these notes on prevention are derived from the field study of victim reaction in Exeter. Figure 1 also immediately suggests ways of increasing difficulties for shoplifters. In terms of this presentation, prevention can best occur when the number of blockages in the flow chart is increased.

Preventing shoplifting

1. *Background*

A. Shopkeepers must recognise the existence of the serious problem posed by shoplifting. There is no cause for complacency if they themselves have not yet been affected by it so far; regrettably, there is every reason to suppose that they will be in the future. If they have a current shoplifting problem, then unless action is taken they can expect it to increase.

B. Shoplifting is a crime, and the police are only too anxious to help control it with the co-operation of the public. The police focus is preventative where possible, since (among other things) this is more practical and less labour-intensive than coming in after the event. Crime prevention officers who can advise on the best ways of increasing protection and preventing shoplifting are attached to all police forces, and their advice is free and readily given. The shopkeeper should take advantage of this service, and aim to prevent shoplifting before it occurs, rather than thinking only about efficient capture of practising shoplifters.

2. *Staffing*

A. Shop staff are a very expensive item on a shopkeeper's account, but their value in frustrating the shoplifter is high.[3] If the shoplifting problem is sizeable, then it would be as well not to consider further reductions in the number of staff available (by, for example, withdrawing 'bundlers' at checkouts in a supermarket, and just leaving 'ringers', thereby making it much easier for shoplifters to slip through).

B. Care should be taken to ensure that there are not times in the day when the shop is excessively denuded of staff (for example, at lunch-time).

C. Every attempt should be made to retain known, trusted staff (through, for example, extra inducements such as differential commission), who will not only reduce the likelihood of staff theft, but will also have greater anti-shoplifting value.

D. Staff should be made aware of the very real probability of their having contact with shoplifters, and should appreciate the need for vigilance that stops short of pestering customers. The pro-

cedure for dealing with shoplifters should be carefully explained to them. It should be remembered that high staff cover represents the best means of preventing shoplifting.
E. It is most important that if a store detective is employed in the shop he should spend as many hours as possible on the shop-floor, and should not be employed in unnecessary travelling or administration. (Where such detectives are employed, their own record of trustworthiness should be carefully checked by references, of course.)
F. Shops of a similar type to each other, and operating in close proximity, could well consider grouping together to share the services of a detective, if an individual shop would be unable to afford the exclusive use of one.

3. *Shop structure and display*

A. The interior of the shop should be well and evenly lit (without excess darkness, shadow or glare), and should be as uncluttered as possible (by, for example, wide pillars, or imitation trees).
B. The shop should have as few entrances and exits as is compatible with local fire regulations.
C. Well-sited, clearly visible, raised observation places, giving a good view of the whole shop, can be expected to have good deterrent value.
D. High-value goods should not be placed on open display at all. (Sample high-value goods can be kept under glass in showcases.) It should only be possible for customers to handle high-value items with the help of a shop assistant.
E. Cheap items should be kept at the front of the shop, and more expensive ones should be kept at the back of the shop, near the office, where they can more easily be kept under close observation. If expensive items are kept at the front of the shop, not only may they be hard to oversee, but also if a shoplifter does steal one as he leaves the shop, he is likely to have that much more of a time advantage over the assistant, who will probably have to come from the rear of the shop to pursue him.
F. No goods for sale should be kept close to exits or entrances; doing otherwise makes it easy for people to steal as they leave the shop, or for people in the street to reach in through the open shop-door and grab items.

G. Items on display in the shop's windows should be of low value only, or they should be dummies or replicas, clearly marked as such. (This is to reduce the chances of a man in the street cutting or smashing his way through the window glass to get at what he thinks are high-value goods.)
H. The height of free-standing displays should be kept to a bare minimum, and should never exceed 1·52 m (5 ft), otherwise the activities of customers standing behind such displays cannot be easily observed by assistants.
I. If possible, displays should be so arranged that when items have been removed for any reason this can be easily verified from a distance of a few metres. Casual displays of jumbled goods make this more difficult.

4. *Stock Control*

A. Where possible stock control should be tightened up, for example, by having unit stock control by which a ticket kept with each item's stock indicates at any time the quantity held.
B. If possible stock should be removed from the stock-room to the shop floor without unpacking or unwrapping it first in the stock-room. This reduces the opportunities for staff to pilfer.
C. More frequent stock-taking, involving of course more work, makes it easier to identify losses, and to pinpoint particularly vulnerable lines.

5. *Control technology*

A. Mirrors have good anti-shoplifting value for two reasons. Not only do they extend the field of vision of the assistant, but also they reduce the amount of blind-space within which the shoplifter can operate freely without being seen, which should function as a deterrent. They should be fixed so as to give the maximum vision combined with minimum need for movement by assistants. As well as large circular corner mirrors, if there are any *necessary* obstructions within a shop (which cannot be removed for structural reasons), such as supporting pillars, these can usefully have mirrors affixed to them.
B. Notices to possible shoplifters indicating the shop's awareness of the likelihood of the crime and disapproval of it can reason-

ably be expected to be seen and read by most people contemplating shoplifting, and ideally there should be a number of these notices.

C. Alarm systems are chiefly of use for giving overall store protection at night from breaking and entering, or for daytime protection of particular parts of the shop, or showcases within it. The range of intrusion detectors now available is extremely good, so is their quality and flexibility of use. Systems can be purchased ready-made, or in kit form from vendors of burglar alarms. Among the types of security systems available are vibration detection systems, which give automatic warning of any vibrations in the shop, caused by movement of a person; infra-red detectors, which are activated by a person's body heat; and microwave motion sensors, with adjustable (highly directional) energy fields which detect all movement in the protected area, to mention but a few. Such systems are available with links direct to the local police station, or to camera surveillance equipment (to take photographs of intruders), or to automatic telephone diallers (using pre-recorded messages), as well as employing standard bell alarms. Most of these devices are tamper-proof, and are designed so as to be incapable of being activated by anything other than a person (such as a small mammal). They are, however, expensive.

D. Good, systematic communications links with neighbouring shops should be arranged for mutual protection, so that advance warning of the operation of shoplifters can be rapidly and unambiguously given and received.

6. *Apprehending shoplifters*

A. Fiber (1972, pp. 250–1) gives a compact version of the essential advice. He states, 'To sustain a legal action against a customer for shoplifting it is usually necessary to prove that the goods were taken away, that no payment was offered and that there was intent to avoid payment. It is therefore always advisable to wait until the suspect has left the shop before making the accusation, otherwise they may claim they intended to pay before leaving.'

7. *Sales policy*

A. The shop which operates a policy of using shop assistants to serve its customers is unlikely to be much affected by shoplifting.
B. It is extremely unwise for small shops to allow themselves to be tempted into having 'supermarket' style conversions, since these are likely to lead to drastic increases in amounts of shoplifting, which may not be compensated for by increased profits.
C. Shops operating self-service sales policies should give serious thought as to the advisability of continuing to do so, especially if they are in an area already hard-hit by shoplifting. It is not always the case that the customer expects and demands self-service. For example in jewellers' shops, tobacconists' and butchers' shops, customers are perfectly prepared to be served. It is unquestionably the case that the presence of self-service sales policies leads to greater shoplifting than would otherwise occur. Goods kept in boxes, under glass in show-cases and on shelves behind the assistant are less vulnerable to theft and *will* still be purchased, and this type of organisation need be no more wasteful of staff time than having quantities of goods chained together to prevent theft which have to be frequently unlocked and replaced.

Envoi

The ideal would be if there were to be an overnight change in customer morality with regard to shoplifting. Since this will not happen, shopkeepers should realistically accept what can be expected, and plan to take what action they reasonably can to make their own particular shop unattractive to, and unrewarding for, shoplifters. Preventing shoplifting is less a question of costly and elaborate technology than it is of recalling the hard lessons learnt by the shopkeepers of the past. There will always be *some* shoplifting, as long as there are shops, but it does not *need* to be on the scale that we have now sadly become so familiar with.

Notes and References

Chapter 1

1 The Anglo-Saxon word *sceoppa* meaning a booth (or stall) is in fact the origin of the word 'shop'.

2 A good description of current anti-theft technology is contained in Wels (1975).

3 Shops with windows like these were much darker inside than the modern shop, since they neither had powerful artificial illumination, nor wide glass windows. The degree of darkness in these emporia must have helped the thief, and concomitantly the degree of light in a modern shop must make the thief's task harder. The 'boutique' type of shop has reverted to the level of illumination of earlier shops as a sales gimmick, through choice rather than necessity, and presumably thereby increased its shoplifting as a result.

4 Lambert (1938) has documented interestingly the development of the department store as a new shop form.

5 Drawn from *Business Monitor* Report on the Census of Distribution and Other Services 1971. Part 13, Retail Organisation Tables and Service Trades, pp. 13/163–13/164.

6 Jefferys is also the author of a valuable book on the functioning of the distributive tradês, *Retailing Trading in Britain 1850–1950* (1954).

7 Cherriman and Wilson (1962) describe the workings of the self-service shop.

8 So many and various are the stimuli to which the modern shopper is subjected that the end product must be self-defeating, in that, faced with so many, most people would tend to try and ignore them, rather than trying hard to listen to them and absorb them. This means that there is a greater emphasis on stridency rather than content of the message, which is equally self-defeating.

9 Dichter (1964), and Engel (1968), in their works show the amount of effort that has gone into studies of consumer motivation.

10 The appallingly harsh conditions of shop workers in Victorian times is well described by Whitaker (1973).

11 Customers find this assumed reverie more often than not exasperating, rather than seeing it as an attempt to combat fatigue and boredom, and it is a source of friction between customer and assistant.

12 This is Clemmer's term (1940, pp. 244–7).

13 Chapman states (1968, p. 165): 'The aim of the display system of the supermarket is to make the taking of goods as easy as possible and to stimulate demand by every possible device up to the limit of the customer's capacity to pay. Since this capacity varies and customers' susceptibility to theft is not always a function of their incomes, these techniques increase thefts and sales together.'

Chapter 2

1   *The Oxford English Dictionary* (1933, vol. IX p. 737 col. 3). An earlier account of the crime of shoplifting in 1597, which does not actually use the term 'shoplifting', but describes the process then current, is contained in Judges (1930, p. 170).

2   The need to pass 10 William III in 1698 gives some indication that shoplifting had been a problem for some time beforehand. Some notion of why is given by Davis (1966, p. 108), who mentions that the congregation of goldsmiths in Cheapside in London in the early seventeenth century was effectively destroyed by shoplifters. In the face of organised teams of shoplifters who 'heaved many a booth', the goldsmiths fled to different parts of the town, until in 1629 Charles I ordered them to return. Hayward indicates (1927, p. 375) that in 1726 the crime of shoplifting had reached a new peak in popularity (Daniel Defoe has depicted the activities of one shoplifter of this period, in his portrayal of Moll Flanders), and in the London of the 1770s, Davis tells us (1966, p. 193): '. . . shoplifting was the commonest of crimes even in small, one room shops where little was put on display which indicates that the shopkeeper's back was turned a good deal while he hunted for goods'.

3   Romilly's diaries were published by his sons in 1840.

4   The absurd cruelty of such laws is revealed in a list of children sentenced to death at the Old Bailey cited by Knell (1965, p. 206). The following offenders found guilty of shoplifting are mentioned in this list:

Name	Age	Crime	Year executed
Weskett	10	shoplifting 12*s*. (60p)	1801
Mary Crawley	10	shoplifting 40*s*. (£2)	1807
John Barney	9	shoplifting 10*s*. (50p)	1816
Chas. Elliott	9	shoplifting 20*s*. (£1)	1820

5   Shoplifting, because it is usually committed alone for the benefit of the individual alone, in a similar way to prostitution, has never developed a complex slang or argot, because practitioners do not require such cant to enable them to communicate with each other secretly in public, because this is not a part of the crime. Such slang as has developed, such as the words 'kettle bagger' (watch thief), 'hoister' (shoplifter), and 'screwsman' (shopbreaker), almost certainly dates from this time.

6   Small, one-pint beer mugs were called 'kittens' and large, two-pint mugs, the normal measure for the period, were called 'cats'. Men who stole mugs were known as 'cat burglars'. The original cat burglar was not possessed of the legendary climbing skill with which he later came to be associated.

7   *The Times*, 20 January 1877, p.11 col. 6.

8   Chief Constable's *Annual Report for Devon And Cornwall Constabulary* (1975, pp. 49, 53).

9   Amazing feats of concealment have been known using specially prepared clothing or bags and boxes carried by the shoplifter, but these are becoming increasingly rare. Presumably the reason is that with so many opportunities to steal in self-service shops this gadgetry is considered unnecessary.

10   If inexperienced assistants have been hired for the expected holiday rushes at Easter, August and Christmas, for example.

11   Lang says (1881, p. 47): 'The papers call lady shoplifters Kleptomaniacs.'

12   It is an often made point, but a very important one, that we are in modern society expecting a very great deal in terms of performance from our citizens, and

these standards are continually being raised, thereby stepping up the level of required performance of an ordinary member of our society, and also creating more 'inadequacy' artificially at the same time.

13 Discussing the role of depression in causing shoplifting, Woddis says (1957, p. 89): 'Of 338 cases of shoplifting referred to the Chicago Psychiatric Institute, 313 were females and no less than 77 per cent showed definable nervous disorder of which mild depression was the most frequent.'

14 Sparks (1966) gives some interesting information on personality disorders among shoplifters.

15 Taking the term 'socialisation' here to mean the acquisition of pro-social norms and values, a restricted definition.

16 'During World War II literally tens of thousands of people refused to leave their homeland because they felt they could not leave their possessions behind. They were eventually caught and immediately killed or dragged off into concentration camps and punished because of their infantile attachment to tangible, hard, security-giving but actually deadly things and objects' (Dichter (1964, p. 4)).

17 Rubin, an adherent of the 1960s Yippy movement, says, for example, 'shop-lifting gets you high!' (1970, p. 122).

18 Before the First World War English society accepted 'the game' and 'the sport', in their spontaneous, 'spectator-free' form, in a far more realistic way, as a temporary and welcome break in the serious business of life and its routine. Since then 'games' have become far more stylised and brittle, allowing less scope for individual action, and concomitantly there are less times when games of any sort are appropriate, (excepting the ritualised games which take place in special arenas, watched by thousands).

19 A number of shops may group together informally with the impetus coming from the police, for mutual aid and protection against professional shoplifters, and arrange to telephone each other, if they become aware of any of these operating in the vicinity.

Chapter 3

1 We still know too little about the role of the victim in relation to crime, although the recent collection of papers by Drapkin (1975) indicates a gradual change in this.

2 Thaw points out (1963, p. 38) that one large combine, Marks & Spencer, in fact gave up elaborate systems of stock control when they found that the costs of administering this were greater than the losses by theft.

3 The Chief Constable's *Annual Report for Devon and Cornwall Constabulary* (1975, pp. 56–7).

4 Wadsworth (1975) gives an interesting break-down of children's crime, and their relative preferences for different forms of it.

5 The presumption would be that the opposite is true for pickpocketing, since it is presumably much easier for thieves to pick other people's pockets in the summer, when the victim is wearing single-layered clothing and wallets and purses suddenly become more accessible and visible, than in the winter months, when multi-layered clothing would make for access difficulties from the pickpocket's point of view.

6 Borrell (1975) suggests that temptation offered in self-service shops constitutes the greatest single pressure to shoplift. Johnson says (1974, p. 43): 'The greater prevalence of large-scale self-service retail establishments has aggravated the difficulties of controlling shoplifting because there is greater public tolerance of thefts from large organisations and easy access to goods is provided.' In addition, Chapman

(1968, p. 165) says: 'The rapid growth of the number of offences of shoplifting which has accompanied the opening of supermarkets . . . illustrates the causal role of the victim.'

7 Ditton (1977) has described in great detail the means used by staff to pilfer in one particular trade, the bakery business, and Hartung (1950), in another, the wholesale meat industry.

Chapter 4

1 Poole (1969, p. 308), in discussing shoplifting in Exeter, does however show that during the period 1950–65 Exeter's average level of shoplifting was considerably greater than the average for all England and Wales.

2 Chapman states (1968, p. 165): 'Informal discussions with retail-trade executives have revealed a tendency to approach the problem first of all as an economic one. Open display and its accompanying sales promotion will pay up to the point where the increase of loss from theft exceeds the increased profit from higher sales . . . . The causal role of the victim is clear.'

3 In August 1977 the Association for the Prevention of Theft, estimating a total annual loss through shoplifting in 1978 of £650 million began a campaign against the shoplifter, the keystone of which was to reward shop assistants with bonuses in the event of their catching shoplifters. Leaving aside the possibility of false arrests and accusations and customer molestation, such a policy (which some shops have already had in operation for many years) is no substitute for a sufficiency of staff.

Bibliography

ADBURGHAM, A. (1964), *Shops and Shopping* (London: Allen & Unwin).
ASPINALL, A., and SMITH, E. A. (eds) (1959), *English Historical Documents*, vol. XI (1783–1832) (London: Eyre & Spottiswoode).
BELSON, W. A. (1969), *The Extent of Stealing by London Boys and Some of Its Origins* (reprint series of the Survey Research Centre, London School of Economics, no. 39).
BOOTH, C. (ed.) (1889–1902), *Life and Labour of the People of London*, 17 vols (London: Macmillan).
BORRELL, C., and CASHINELLA, B. (1975), *Crime in Britain Today* (London: Routledge & Kegan Paul).
BRADLEY, M., and FENWICK, D. (1975), *Shopping Habits and Attitudes to Shop Hours in Great Britain* (London: H.M.S.O.).
CAMERON, M. O. (1964), *The Booster and the Snitch* (New York: Free Press of Glencoe).
CARTER, R. L. (1974), *Theft in the Market*, Hobart Paper no. 60 (London: The Institute of Economic Affairs).
CHAPMAN, D. (1968), *Sociology and the Stereotype of the Criminal* (London: Tavistock).
CHERRIMAN, L. A., and WILSON, R. (1962), *The Operation of a Self-Service Store* (Loughborough: Co-operative Union).
CHESNEY, K. (1972), *The Victorian Underworld* (Harmondsworth: Penguin).
CLEMMER, D. (1940), *The Prison Community* (Boston: Christopher Publishing House).
COWIE, J., and COWIE, V. (1968), *Delinquency in Girls* (London: Heinemann).
CROOKSTON, P. (1967), *Villain* (London: Cape).
DALTON, K. (1960), 'Schoolgirls' Behaviour and Menstruation', *British Medical Journal*, 2, pp. 1647–716.
DAVIS, D. (1966), *A History of Shopping* (London: Routledge & Kegan Paul).
DAWSON, W. S. (5th ed., 1946), *Aids to Psychiatry* (London: Baillière Tindall & Cox).
DEBUYST, Cn, LEJOUR, G., and RACINE, A. (1960), *Petits Voleurs de grand magasins* (Brussels: Centre d'Étude de la Delinquance Juvenile, A.S.B.S. publication no. 5).
DICHTER, E. (1964), *Handbook of Consumer Motivations: The Psychology of the World of Objects* (New York: McGraw-Hill).
DITTON, J. (1977), *Part-time Crime: An Ethnography of Fiddling and Pilferage* (London: Macmillan).
DRAPKIN, I., and VIANO, E. (eds) (1975), *Victimology: A New Focus*, 5 vols (Lexington, Mass.: D. C. Heath & Co.).

EDWARDS, A. T. (1933), *The Architecture of Shops* (London: Chapman & Hall).
EDWARDS, L. E. E. (1958), *Shoplifting and Shrinkage Protection for Stores* (Springfield, Ill.: Charles C. Thomas).
ENGEL, J. F., KOLLAT, D.T., and BLACKWELL, R. D. (1968), *Consumer Behaviour* (Hinsdale, Ill.: Dryden Press).
FIBER, A. (1972), *The Complete Guide to Retail Management* (Harmondsworth: Penguin).
GIBBENS, T. C. N., and PRINCE, J. (1962), *Shoplifting* (London: The Institute for the Study and Treatment of Delinquency).
GIBBONS, D. C. (1968), *Society, Crime and Criminal Careers* (Englewood Cliffs, N.J.: Prentice-Hall).
HARTUNG, F. E. (1950), 'Whitecollar Offences in the Wholesale Meat Industry in Detroit', *American Journal of Sociology*, 56, pp. 25–35.
HAYWARD, A. L. (ed.) (1927), *Lives of the Most Remarkable Criminals* (London: G. Routledge & Sons).
HEAD, R., and KIRKMAN, F. (1928), *The English Rogue* (London: G. Routledge & Sons).
HOME OFFICE (1973), *Shoplifting and Thefts by Shop Staff: Report of a Working Party on Internal Shop Security* (London: H.M.S.O.).
JACKSON, R. L. (5th ed., 1962), *Criminal Investigation* (London: Sweet & Maxwell).
JEFFERYS, J. B. (1954), *Retail Trading in Britain 1850–1950* National Institute of Economic and Social Research, Economic and Social Studies no. 13 (Cambridge University Press).
— (1973), 'Distributive Trades', *Chambers Encyclopedia*, 4, pp. 561–5.
JOHNSON, E. H. (1974), *Crime, Correction and Society* (Homewood, Ill.: The Dorsey Press).
JUDGES, A. V. (1930), *The Elizabethan Underworld* (London: G. Routledge & Sons).
KNELL, B. E. F. (1965), 'Capital Punishment: Its Administration in Relation to Juvenile Offenders in the Nineteenth Century and Its Possible Administration in the Eighteenth Century', *British Journal of Criminology*, 5, pp. 198–207.
LAMBERT, R. S. (1938), *The Universal Provider: A Study of William Whiteley and the Rise of the London Department Store* (London: Harrap).
LANG, A. (1881), *The Library* (London: Macmillan).
LEVY, H. (1947), *The Shops of Britain: A Study in Retail Distribution* (London: Kegan Paul).
MCCLELLAND, W. G. (1962), 'The Supermarket and Society', *Sociological Review*, 10, pp. 133–44.
MCINTOSH, M. (1971), 'Changes in the Organization of Thieving', in *Images of Deviance*, ed. S. Cohen (Harmondsworth: Penguin) pp. 98–133.
MAIR, G. I. U. (1976), 'Towards a Sociology of Shopping' (M.Sc. thesis, University of Strathclyde).
MATZA, D. (1964), *Delinquency and Drift* (New York: Wiley).
MAYHEW, H. (1861–2), *London Labour and the London Poor*, 2 vols (London: Griffin Bohn).
MILLER, W. B. (1958), 'Lower-Class Culture as a Generating Milieu of Gang Delinquency' *Journal of Social Issues*, 14, pp. 5–19.
NATIONAL ECONOMIC DEVELOPMENT OFFICE (1971), *The Future Pattern of Shopping* (London: H.M.S.O.).
PARKER, T., and ALLERTON, R. (1962), *The Courage of His Convictions* (London: Hutchinson).
PITTMAN, D. J., and GORDON, W. (1958), *Revolving Door* (New York: Free Press of Glencoe).

POOLE, A. R. (1969), 'Aspects of Crime in Exeter 1900–65', in *Exeter and Its Region*, ed. F. Barlow (University of Exeter) pp. 302–14.
ROWNTREE, B. S. (1902), *Poverty: A Study of Town Life* (London: Macmillan).
RUBIN, J. (1970), *Do It!* (New York: Simon & Schuster).
SCHIPKOVENSKY, N. (1965), 'Athérosclerosé cérébrale et criminalité', *Revue internationale de criminologie et de police technique*, 19, pp. 51–62.
SCHUR, E. M. (1965), *Crimes without Victims* (Englewood Cliffs, N.J.: Prentice-Hall).
SLATER, E., and ROTH, M. (1970), *Clinical Psychiatry* (London: Baillière, Tindall & Cox).
SOMAKE, E. E., and HELLBERG, R. (1956), *Shops and Stores To-day, Their Design, Planning and Organisation* (London: Batsford).
SPARKS, R. F. (1966), 'The Decision to Remand for Mental Examination', *British Journal of Criminology*, 6, pp. 6–26.
STUTT, H. (1965), 'Das Blutzuckermangel-Syndrom in seiner forensischen Bedeutung', *Monatsschrift fur Kriminologie und Shafrechtsreform*, 48, pp. 67–88.
THAW, L. (1963), 'No Ledgers for St. Michaels', *Aspect*, no. 7.
WADSWORTH, M. E. J. (1975), 'Delinquency in a National Sample of Children', *British Journal of Criminology*, 15, pp. 167–74.
WALSH, D. P. (1969), 'The Social Adjustment of the Physically Handicapped with Special Reference to Their Crime and Deviance' (Ph.D. thesis, University of London).
WHITAKER, W. B. (1973), *Victorian and Edwardian Shopworkers* (Newton Abbot: David & Charles).
WILLAN, T. S. (1970), *An Eighteenth-Century Shopkeeper: Abraham Dent of Kirkby Stephen* (Manchester University Press).
WELS, B. (1975), *Fire and Theft Security Systems* (Slough: Foulsham-Tab Ltd).
WODDIS, G. M. (1957), 'Depression and Crime', *British Journal of Delinquency*, **8**, pp. 85–94.
YOSHIMASU, S. (1965), 'Zwei Falle von Brandstifung beim prodromalen Stadium der Huntintonschen Chorea', *Acta Criminologiae et Medicinae Legalis Japonica*, **31**, pp. 25—31.

Index

Adburgham 17
advertising 40
age of offenders, *see* offenders
alarms, *see* prevention
amount stolen, *see* offences
Annual Abstract of Statistics 9
area distribution of offences, *see* offences
Aristotle 54
Aspinall and Smith 23
automated shops, *see* shops

bag-checkouts 88
Barrett 24
Belson 35, 57
Booth 25
Bradley and Fenwick 17

Cameron 35, 57, 75
capitalism 41
Carter 57
causes, *see* motives
caution, the 76
Census of Distribution 1971 5
cerebral arteriosclerosis 37
Chesney 25–6
Chief Constable's *Annual Report for Devon and Cornwall* 74
children 19, 28, 39, 42, 67, 69, 70, 91
closed circuit TV, *see* prevention
communication systems, *see* prevention

communism, *see* motives
community disposal of offenders, *see* offenders
community response to 47–51
counter service 7, 10, 14, 20, 21, 46, 54, 59, 62, 76, 78, 80, 81, 82, 85, 87, 91, 92, 93, 94, 97, 100
courts 48, 52, 82, 94, 95, 96
Cowie 36
crime-prevention officers 107
Crookston 49

daily distribution of offences, *see* offences
Dalton 37
Davis 1, 4, 6, 10, 17
Dawson 36
Debuyst 69
department stores, *see* shops
depression 37
detection, rate of, *see* offences
detectives, *see* security staff
Devon and Cornwall 31
diabetes 37
discount houses, *see* shops
display and prevention, *see* prevention
display stands 86, 109
disposal of offenders, *see* offenders

early warning telephone systems 43, 75, 87

Edwards 1
Ellison 26
empty time 97, 98, 101, 105
Engel 17
escape routes 33, 54, 86, 98–9, 102, 105
Exeter 57, 90
  shoplifting in 61–76

fairs 1
fall-backs 98–9, 102, 105
Fiber 7, 110
fines 52–3, 76
fun-ethic 42

game motive, *see* motive
Gibbens 35, 57, 69, 75
Gibbons 93
glass 3–4, 85, 88, 111
goods selected for theft, *see* offences
greed, *see* motives

habitual offenders, *see* offenders
Head and Kirkman 23
history 23–8
Home Office Study 57
Huguenots 3
Huntington's chorea 37
hypotheses, *see* survey

ideological motives, *see* motives
impulse purchase 32, 55, 85, 96
infra-red detectors 110
intrusion detectors 110

Jackson 44
Jefferys 6–7
jewellers 3, 27, 45, 63–4, 73, 87

King William's Act, 1698 23–4
Kirkman 23
kleptomania 36

Larceny Act, 1916 28
Levy 1

McClelland 20
McIntosh 43
Mackintosh, Sir James 25
'mail-order' shoplifting, *see* offenders
Mair 17
market stall 1–3, 63–4
markets 1–4
Marx 41
materialism 40
Matza 43
Mayhew 25
media 47, 49, 50, 58, 101–2
medieval times 1–3
menstrual cycle 37
mental illness 36–7, 99
methods used
  by offenders 69–72
  in survey 58–61
microwave motion sensors 110
Miller 41
mirrors, *see* prevention
'mixed service' 59, 62, 76, 78, 81, 82, 91, 92, 111
monthly variations 64–5
motives 35–46, 99, 103
  communism 41
  game 41–3
  greed 40–1, 81
  ideological 41

Newgate 24
notices, *see* prevention

occupation of offenders, *see* offenders
offences
  amount stolen 72–3, 74
  area distribution of 30, 61–2
  daily distribution of 64–6

detection, rate of 63–4
extent and concentration 61–7
goods selected for theft 72, 94
occurrence of last-known 62–3
records 60–1
seasonal variations in 64, 72
timing 64–7
offenders 26–7, 28, 31–5, 75
age of 68
amount stolen by 72–3, 74
characteristics of 67–76
detected 91
disposal of 52–3, 76–7
goods selected for theft 72, 94
habitual offenders 99
'mail-order' offenders 75
method used by 69–72, 91
occupation of 68–9
personality disorder in 37
preference for ganging 69–70
previous crime 75–6
professionalism among 60, 73–75, 87, 93
sample of 59–60
senility among 37
sex of 67

Parker and Allerton 48
physical assault 79, 82
physical states 37–8
Pittman and Gordon 68
police 17, 31, 35, 37, 43, 44, 47–8, 55, 57, 59, 60, 78, 83, 93, 95, 96, 107
poverty 38–9, 81
pregnancy 37
premises where offences occur 63
prepackaging 6, 32, 84
prevention of 51, 84–9, 107–11
alarms 3, 87, 109–10
closed circuit T.V. 35, 82, 88
communication systems 87, 110
display by 86, 108–9

mirrors 79, 87, 109
notices 35, 82, 87, 109
previous criminality of offenders, *see* offenders
Prince Regent 24
prison 52–3, 76, 95
probation 52
professional shoplifting 43–5, 73–5
punishment 42

radar sentries 3
rationality 99
recognition of shoplifters 79–80
reporting 67, 91
research methods, *see* survey
retail buying groups 6
retail establishments, *see* shops
ring-switching 27
Romilly 23–5
Rowntree 38
Rutherford, Dame Margaret 50

sales policy 84, 92, 94, 111
Schipkovensky 37
security staff 78, 83, 87, 108
self-selection 6, 12
self-service 6–8, 10, 12, 15, 59, 62, 70, 78–9, 80–5, 88, 91–5, 97, 100, 111
senility, *see* offenders
sex of offenders, *see* offenders
shop assistant 6–7, 12, 19, 33–4, 63, 85, 93
role of 12–17
supermarket assistants 12–16
theft by 83, 85
shopkeepers 7, 21, 37, 43, 45
action taken to prevent shoplifting 76–9
awareness of shoplifting 80–3
moral inconsistency 96–7
opinions as to cause of shoplifting 80–1

shopkeepers – *contd*
  recognition of shoplifters 79–80
  response to shoplifting 76, 78, 79
  sample of 58–9
shoplifters, *see* offenders
shoplifting prevention, *see* prevention
shopping 17–20, 22, 46
shopping custom, social significance of 17–22
shops
  automated 12
  change in type over time 8–12
  department stores 4, 8, 10–12, 16, 20–1, 50, 56, 63–4, 94
  development of 1–8
  discount houses 8
  geography 44, 86
  numbers of 9
  in the sample 58–9
  size and shoplifting 93
  supermarkets 6–8, 63–4 and *passim*
shrinkage 16, 17, 51, 95, 96
Slater and Roth 36–7
social service provision 38
social workers 95
Somake and Hellberg 1
staffing in shops 107–8
stereotypes 49–51
stock control 109
store detectives, *see* security staff
Stutt 37
supermarkets, *see* shops

supermarket assistant, *see* shop assistant
survey
  conclusions 97
  hypotheses 53–6, 92–5
  methods 57–61

television, prevention by closed circuit 35, 82, 88
theft 100–4
Theft Act 1968 28
theft by shop staff 83, 85
ticket-switching 88
Times, The 26
timing of offences, *see* offences
Travelling Criminals Index 75
Trouble in Store 50

vibration detection systems 110
victims 48–9
  availability 100
  precipitation of crime 57, 91, 97
  prevention of 53
  reaction 76–83
voluntary wholesale chains 6

Walsh 37
Wellington, Duke of 95
wholesalers 58
Willan 1
William's Act, King, 1698 23–4

Yoshimasu 37
youthfulness 39